Anonymous

Model Notes of Lessons

For Class Teaching

Anonymous

Model Notes of Lessons
For Class Teaching

ISBN/EAN: 9783337179618

Printed in Europe, USA, Canada, Australia, Japan

Cover: Foto ©Paul-Georg Meister /pixelio.de

More available books at **www.hansebooks.com**

Royal School Series.

MODEL
NOTES OF LESSONS.

FOR CLASS TEACHING.

OISE/UT LIBRARY

London:
T. NELSON AND SONS, PATERNOSTER ROW;
EDINBURGH; AND NEW YORK.

1880.

PREFACE.

This is a book for Pupil Teachers and for Students in Training Colleges. It covers the whole ground of ordinary elementary instruction—Reading, Writing, and Arithmetic; Object Lessons; History and Geography; Grammar and Analysis. Of the specific subjects it includes the two most commonly taken—English Literature and Domestic Economy. Chapters on Morals and on Scripture have been added, in order to adapt the book to all classes of schools.

The book differs from others on the same subject in being at once a manual of method and a collection of models. The latter will be found to be characterized by great variety, both in subject and in system of arrangement.

In a recent Government Examination Paper the following directions on this subject are given:—

"*N.B.*—Make them real notes of a LESSON, not a string of names, but well arranged particulars clearly explained, in the order most likely to interest children and help them to remember. Do not lose time in speaking of the apparatus needed, &c., &c., but get at once into the lesson itself."

The three aims here specified—arranging the matter, interesting the class, and aiding the memory—have been kept prominently in view in compiling the following pages; and they are offered to Teachers with confidence, in the belief that they will be found really helpful in one of the most important and most difficult parts of school work.

CONTENTS.

INTRODUCTION.

WHAT ARE NOTES OF LESSONS?.. 9

CHAPTER I.

NOTES OF LESSONS ON ANIMALS... 14
Model Lesson: The Lion... 16
Comparison of Animals:—
   Horse—Ostrich—Cod... 17
Exercises:—
   The Camel—The Crocodile—The Wolf—The Whale—The Rattlesnake—
   The Eagle—The Frog—The Ant—Additional Subjects 18

CHAPTER II.

NOTES OF LESSONS ON PLANTS 20
Model Lesson: The Mahogany Tree 22
Comparison of Plants:—
   Oak—Tea Plant—Potato.. 23
Exercises:—
   The Daisy—The Elm—The Sugar Cane—The Birch—The Primrose—The
   Coffee Tree—The Common Orange—The Rice Plant—Additional Subjects 24

CHAPTER III.

NOTES OF LESSONS ON MINERALS.. 26
Model Lesson: Iron 28
Comparison of Minerals:—
   Gold—Marble—Coal... 29
Exercises:—
   Silver—Salt—Clay—The Diamond—Chalk—Slate—Additional Subjects..... 30

vi   CONTENTS.

CHAPTER IV.

Notes of Lessons on Manufactured Articles... 32
Model Lesson : English Coins... 33
Comparison of Manufactured Articles :—
    Glass—Paper—A Steel Pen... 34
Exercises :—
    A Needle—Leather—Bread—Woollen Cloth—Oil—A Bell—Glue—Steam—
    Additional Subjects.. 35

CHAPTER V.

Notes of Lessons on Reading.. 37
Model Lesson : Prose Reading... 40
Model Lesson : Poetical Reading... 41

CHAPTER VI.

Notes of Lessons on Writing... 42
Model Lesson : Writing.. 45

CHAPTER VII.

Notes of Lessons on Arithmetic... 46
Model Lesson : Simple Subtraction.. 50
Model Lesson : Reduction of Money... 51
Model Lesson : The Vulgar Fraction.. 52

CHAPTER VIII.

Notes of Lessons on Grammar... 53
Model Lesson : The Noun... 58
Comparison of Parts of Speech :—
    The Verb—The Adjective—The Pronoun....................................... 59
Model Lesson : The Parts of Speech... 60
Model Lesson : The Complex Sentence... 61

CHAPTER IX.

Notes of Lessons on History... 62
Model Lesson : A Reign—Edward I... 65
Comparison of Reigns :—
    Elizabeth—Charles I.—William III. and Mary II............................. 66

Exercises: Reigns:—
    Alfred—Richard I.—Henry VII.. 67
Model Lesson: A Battle—Quebec.. 68
Comparison of Battles:—
    Bannockburn—Nile—Waterloo.. 69
Exercises: Battles:—
    Agincourt—Spanish Armada—Plassey... 70
Model Lesson: A Biography—Livingstone... 71
Comparison of Biographies:—
    Milton—Nelson—Watt.. 72
Exercises: Biographies:—
    Sir Walter Ralegh—William Shakespeare—Sir Walter Scott.............. 73

CHAPTER X.

NOTES OF LESSONS ON GENERAL GEOGRAPHY.. 74
Model Lesson: A Country—England... 78
Comparison of Countries:—
    Ireland—France—Canada... 79
Exercises: Countries:—
    Scotland—Palestine—India... 80
Model Lesson: A City—London.. 81
Comparison of Cities:—
    Glasgow—Delhi—Metz.. 82
Exercises: Cities:—
    Edinburgh—Dublin—Jerusalem.. 83
Model Lesson: A Mountain Range—The Alps... 84
Comparison of Mountain Ranges:—
    Grampians—Andes—Himalaya... 85
Exercises: Mountain Ranges:—
    Pyrenees—Apennines—Balkans—Ural Mountains............................ 86
Model Lesson: A River—The Nile.. 87
Comparison of Rivers:—
    Thames—Volga—Amazon.. 88
Exercises: Rivers:—
    Ganges—Severn—St. Lawrence.. 89

CHAPTER XI.

NOTES OF LESSONS ON PHYSICAL GEOGRAPHY... 90
Model Lesson: Form of the Earth.. 94
Model Lesson: A Map... 95
Model Lesson: Climate... 96
Model Lesson: Tides... 97
Exercises:—
    The Seasons—A River—Winds—Additional Subjects......................... 98

CHAPTER XII.

Notes of Lessons on Domestic Economy 100
Model Lesson: Food.. 103
Model Lesson: Ventilation... 104
Exercises :—
    Clothing—Dwellings—Saving or Thrift—Additional Subjects............... 105

CHAPTER XIII.

Notes of Lessons on Morals 106
Model Lesson: Obedience... 108
Comparison of Moral Subjects :—
    Politeness—Gratitude—Forgiveness... 109
Exercises on Morals, &c. :—
    Cruelty to Animals—Punctuality—War—Additional Subjects............... 110

CHAPTER XIV.

Notes of Lessons on Scripture... 111
Model Lesson: A Parable—The Sower.. 114
Comparison of Parables :—
    The Pearl—The Lost Sheep—The True Vine................................... 115
Exercises: Parables :—
    The Tares—The Labourers—The Wicked Husbandmen...................... 116
Model Lesson: A Miracle—The Cripple Healed..................................... 117
Comparison of Miracles :—
    The Sick of the Palsy—The Centurion's Servant—The Widow's Son...... 118
Exercises: Miracles :—
    The Nobleman's Son Healed—Five Thousand Fed—Ten Lepers Cleansed... 119

CHAPTER XV.

General Principles 120

CONCLUSION.

On Giving a Lesson.. 124

MODEL NOTES OF LESSONS

FOR

CLASS TEACHING.

INTRODUCTION.

WHAT ARE NOTES OF LESSONS?

The Notes of a Lesson are the systematic arrangement, generally in a tabular form, of the information which a teacher wishes to impart on a given subject. They are the plan or outline of the lesson he means to give to his class, and they serve the same purpose as heads or a skeleton serve to a preacher or lecturer.

From the preparation of Notes of Lessons the Teacher himself derives great benefit. The exercise enables him to test his own knowledge, and at the same time accustoms him to select and arrange his information. The use of these Notes in teaching gives him a thorough grasp of his subject, which enables him to keep the chief points of the lesson well before his class, and, without loss of time, to take up in their proper order all the divisions and subdivisions of his subject.

The Scholars, however, are the chief gainers when the teacher gives his lessons from well digested Notes. From the outline of the matter sketched on the black-board, they see the whole plan at one view, and are able to understand the relation of each part to the rest. Not only is the understanding aided by this means; it is also a material help to the memory. As the lesson is gradually and systematically unfolded, the minds of the children are expanded and strengthened. While their stock of knowledge is being increased, their powers of observation and comparison are exercised. They are encouraged to use their minds—to think for themselves. In a word, the process is education, and not merely cramming.

The Inspector looks upon Notes of Lessons as one of the best tests of a teacher's practical skill. It is necessary that a teacher should be well informed, but to be the owner of a mass of information is not sufficient; he must also know how to make use of that information for teaching purposes. The possession of building materials and tools will not enable a man to produce a stately or a stable building. He must have a well-arranged plan for his guidance, and it is on the plan that the strength and beauty of the edifice mainly depend. When an inspector asks for notes of a lesson, say on "the Lion," the question really to be answered is not, "What do you know about the lion?" but, "How would you teach what you know about the lion?"

The Notes of a Lesson generally consist of:—

1. THE INTRODUCTION.
2. THE MATTER.
3. THE HEADS.
4. THE METHOD.

1. **The Introduction.**—This may take the form of a reference to some well-known object resembling or suggesting the subject of the lesson. It may take the form of a story or of a few questions. Attention may be directed to a picture, or a map, or to a specimen of the article about which the lesson is to be given. In some instances no introduction is needed, and a simple announcement of the subject is sufficient.

In the Model Lesson on the Lion (page 16), the cat is referred to as an introduction. This is done because the cat is the member of the lion family best known to children, and because almost everything that is said of the one animal may, with modifications, be said of the other. In the same way a lesson on the elephant may be introduced by a reference to the horse; a lesson on the wolf by referring to the dog; and a lesson on the snake by referring to the worm.

For the sake of variety, another plan may be adopted. A reference may be made to some familiar use of the animal or object in question. Thus, a cloth coat might be used to introduce a lesson on the sheep; a piece of cheese or a glass of milk, to introduce a lesson on the cow; a table or a chair, a lesson on a tree; a poker or a nail, a lesson on iron; and a fire, a lesson on coal.

It is desirable that the forms of introduction used by a teacher should be varied; but it is more important that the introduction itself should be apt and natural. The success of a lesson depends in a great measure on the attention of the scholars being arrested at the beginning, and therefore too much importance cannot be attached to this feature.

2. **The Matter.**—This division presents to the eye the whole of the information which it is thought advisable to impart. It is essential that the information be accurate. If it fail in this, it will fail in everything. It should also be adapted to the age and the previous attainments of the children for whom it is intended. That which is suitable for a fifth or a sixth standard would be much too difficult for a first standard, and that which would be within the comprehension of younger children would be of little use to those in a higher grade.

The matter must be interesting. Children do not care to listen to dry details, but descriptions of strange customs, of curious things, of stirring events, and of objects of wonder, at once arrest their attention.

The matter must also be useful. It should not consist of out-of-the-way facts or far-fetched observations, but only of such information as school children are likely to require. To give children information which they cannot assimilate, or which they are not likely to have occasion to recall, is not only a waste of time, it is an abuse of their faculties.

3. **The Heads.**—These are the divisions under which the matter is arranged. They should be as few as possible, quite

distinct from one another, and each should be complete in itself. In giving the lesson, the heads should be written on the black-board.

4. **The Method.**—This consists of suggestions as to how the "matter" may be most effectively communicated. It is not enough that the facts should be stated by the teacher and repeated by the scholars. Various arts and devices must be employed in order to help the minds of the learners to understand and to grasp the thoughts set before them. It is here, indeed, that the highest qualities of the teacher have fullest scope. In addition to simple and formal explanations, he must make use of suggestive comparisons, of striking contrasts, or of familiar illustrations, as may seem most suitable in each case.

Referring again to the Model Lesson on the Lion (page 16), we find the following examples:—Mammal is *explained* as suckling the young; the lion, as a flesh-eater, is *contrasted* with the cow and the horse, which are not flesh-eaters; the sheathed claws of the lion are *compared* with a sword and its sheath; and the strength of the lion is *illustrated* by a story of a lion carrying off an ox.

These examples, like many others found in the following pages, are very simple; but in this lies their value, for simplicity should be the first aim of a teacher in expounding any subject.

Pictures, maps, diagrams, models, and general objects, should be freely used wherever they are appropriate. Every place mentioned should be pointed out on a map. All plans and forms of construction should be sketched on the black-board. Dimensions should be shown by actual measurement, or, when that is impracticable, by comparison. However well known an article may be, either the article itself or a picture of it should be shown during the lesson. Children may have seen or handled an object daily for years, and yet when asked to recall its form and qualities in detail by an act of memory, they are often unable to do so.

When the article itself is shown, the children should have an opportunity of exercising their senses in noting its form and discovering its qualities. Thus *sight* tells us that an orange is round and yellow; *smell* perceives that a rose has an agreeable odour; *hearing* informs us that a note is high or low; *taste* discovers that sugar is sweet, and *touch* that iron is cold and hard.

What has been said of the selection of matter holds good also, and even more strongly, of method: it must be carefully adapted to the different ages and circumstances of the children. Nothing makes a greater demand on the judgment and good sense of the teacher than this. The younger and the less informed his scholars are, the simpler and the more painstaking will be the arts he employs to break down to them the knowledge he wishes to impart. His illustrations and his comparisons must not refer to matters that do not come naturally within the knowledge of the children. To explain the unknown by the unknown is like speaking to children in a strange tongue. This is why it is easier for a teacher to give lessons, on many subjects, to advanced than to very elementary classes. In the case of older scholars the vocabulary is larger, the field which may be drawn upon for illustration is wider, and the mental powers are stronger and more elastic. A good teacher should be able to prepare two or three sets of Notes on the same subject, adapted to different stages; and it would be well if, when specimen Notes are asked from pupil teachers, the standard or the age to which they are applicable were more frequently specified.

NATURAL HISTORY.

CHAPTER I.

NOTES OF LESSONS ON ANIMALS.

ANIMALS form favourite subjects for systematic lessons, even with the youngest scholars. No subject in the school course is better adapted for arousing the interest and holding the attention of children. With some animals they are familiar from their earliest years. With others they are made acquainted by pictures. Their powers of observation are therefore exercised on animals as soon as on any objects in nature. This is a great help to the teacher; and as the objects are interesting in themselves, they may appropriately be chosen as the material for the earliest object-lessons.

The Notes of a Lesson on an Animal may be most conveniently arranged under the following heads:—

     I. CLASSIFICATION.
    II. STRUCTURE.
   III. HABITS AND QUALITIES.
   IV. FOOD.
    V. LOCALITY.
   VI. USES.

I. Classification.—The purpose of this head is to define the position of the particular animal in the Animal kingdom, to show what other animals it is like, and in what it differs from other animals of the same species or kind. This is done most accurately by telling the division, the class, the order, and the tribe to which the animal belongs. We say that the lion is a backboned or vertebrated animal; but that is not enough to mark its position, for birds, reptiles, and fishes are also back-boned. When we have said that the lion is a mammal, or a suckler of its young, we have separated it at once from birds, reptiles, and fishes. But there are many orders of mammals. We therefore say that it is a flesh-eater, to distinguish it from the cow and the horse. But there are several tribes of flesh-eaters; and when we have said that the lion belongs to the cat tribe, we have defined its exact place in the animal kingdom. The student will find it useful to consult a table of the Divisions of the Animal Kingdom. (See "Royal Reader" No. VI., p. 362.)

II. **Structure.**—Under this head we describe the appearance of the animal, both general and particular. Its size, its colour, and its form must be carefully specified. In mentioning its parts, particular notice must be taken of any feature which specially characterizes it—for example, of the trunk in the elephant, of the horn in the rhinoceros, of the paw in the lion, of the pouch in the kangaroo.

III. **Habits.**—This head includes particulars regarding the disposition, mode of life, and characteristic doings of the animal.

IV. **Food.**—This head is important, because of the relation which the animal's food bears to its structure and to its habits.

V. **Locality.**—Under this head it is necessary to mention not only the country or countries in which the animal is found, but also whether it frequents mountains and rocks, or forests, or deserts and open plains. If the animal runs wild in some parts of the world, and is tame in others, let the fact be mentioned.

VI. **Uses.**—The uses, if any, to which the living animal is put are mentioned under this head. It also specifies the purposes to which the parts of its body may be applied after death. In the case of wild animals, the mode of capture may be described. An illustrative anecdote may appropriately close the lesson.

We now give a Model Lesson on the Lion, arranged under the heads just specified; and also the Outlines of three Lessons on Animals of different Structure, &c. From the latter it will be seen that the model may be adapted to any animal.

MODEL LESSON: THE LION.

Articles required.—*Pictures of Cat and Lion—Map of World.*

INTRODUCTION.—Show pictures of Cat and Lion, and ask questions to bring out their likeness.

HEADS.	MATTER.	METHOD.
CLASSIFICATION.	Division.—Back-boned........	Contrast with worm, snail, and star-fish.
	Class.—Mammals..........	Explain literal meaning: "suckling its young." Contrast with birds and fishes.
	Order.—Flesh-eaters	Contrast with cow and horse.
	Family.—Cat tribe..........	Give examples: cat, tiger; and ask for others.
STRUCTURE.	Body.—Long—strong, compact bones—powerful muscles—tawny skin...........	Point to each part of animal when describing it. Get description from the class.
	Size.—Height, about 4 feet—length, about 7 feet......	Show lengths on school-room wall.
	Head.—Round...........	Compare with cat.
	Eyes.—Large, round—able to see in dark...........	Show use, in seeking prey by night. (See HABITS.)
	Teeth.—Sharp-pointed.......	Show use, in tearing flesh. (See FOOD.)
	Tongue.—Rough..........	Show use, in scraping flesh off bones. (See FOOD.)
	Neck.—Very strong........	Illustrate by story of a lion carrying off an ox.
	Mane.—Long—on male only...	Compare with horse's mane.
	Whiskers.—Extend sideways from mouth...........	Show use, in enabling it to feel its way through the jungle.
	Feet.—Padded under each toe..	Show use, when approaching its prey.
	Claws.—Sharp—sheathed in pad	Compare with sword and its sheath.
	Tail.—Long, tufted.........	Compare with tassel.
HABITS and QUALITIES.	Sleeps during day—lies in wait near water at night, and springs on animals as they drink—fierce—cunning—fond of young.	Compare with cat watching for mice, and its mode of catching them.
FOOD.	Beast of prey—deer, sheep, oxen, sometimes men.	Refer to STRUCTURE and HABITS.
LOCALITY.	Africa, India, Persia. Asiatic lion smaller than the African.	Show countries on map.
USES.	Skins used for rugs.	Tell a lion-story: hunted with elephants, &c.

COMPARISON OF ANIMALS.

THIS table contains Outline Lessons on a Quadruped, a Bird, and a Fish, arranged on the same plan, in order to show that the model may be adapted to any animal. The student should be asked to construct a similar skeleton of lessons on other animals, say the Elephant, the Shark, and the Spider. By this means he will become thoroughly acquainted with the structure of the lesson.

Arrangement of Lesson.	HORSE.	OSTRICH.	COD.
INTRODUCTION	*Refer to daily use.*	*Refer to Peacock.*	*Ask for names of well-known fishes.*
CLASSIFICATION.	Division.... Back-boned. Class...... Mammals. Order...... Thick-skinned.	Division.... Back-boned. Class...... Birds. Order...... Runners.	Division.... Back-boned. Class...... Fishes. Order...... Bone-skeleton.
STRUCTURE.	Size—colour—form of body—kinds.	Size—colour—form of body—wings—feathers—legs—feet.	Size—colour—form of body—jaws—teeth—fins.
HABITS and QUALITIES.	In a wild state lives in herds—fleet-footed—very timid.	Lives in flocks—quick of hearing—acute smell—fleet-footed.	Haunts shallow water—spawns in cold seas.
FOOD.	Vegetable: grass—hay—corn—beans.	Vegetable: shrubs—young plants—seeds—almost any kind.	Small fish—worms—crabs and other small shell-fish.
LOCALITY.	In nearly all parts of the world—found wild in South America, in Tartary, and in Africa.	In deserts of Africa.	Chiefly in seas of temperate regions. Very abundant off Newfoundland and Nova Scotia.
USES.	As a domestic animal, is sagacious, obedient, and faithful—skin is used for leather—hoofs for glue—hair for cushions.	Valuable feathers—flesh eaten—eggs used.	Food — very prolific — 15,000 British seamen employed in the cod-fishery.

EXERCISES.

Matter for Notes of Lessons, to be arranged on the plan of the Model Lesson.

THE CAMEL.

Backboned, mammal, cud-chewer—larger than horse, dark brown skin, rough hair, large hump or humps, long neck, small head, long slender legs, soft broad feet, peculiar stomach—chews the cud, needs little water, is very patient, kneels to be loaded and unloaded—eats thorny shrubs, date leaves, beans—Arabia, Africa, South-eastern Europe—beast of burden; milk, flesh, fat, hair.

THE CROCODILE.

Backboned, reptile, scale-covered—twenty feet in length, powerful jaws, saw-like teeth, scale-covered body, back feet five toes, fore feet four toes—basks in the sun, inhabits fresh water, swims swiftly, walks slowly, buries its eggs in the mud—feeds on putrid fish and flesh—Africa and Asia—hunted by natives, used to be worshipped.

THE WOLF.

Backboned, mammal, flesh-eater, dog-tribe—about the size of a large dog, reddish gray hair, long head, pointed nose, fiery eyes, erect ears, bushy tail, strong legs—very cunning, hunts in packs, has acute smell, is very ferocious—eats flesh of all kinds—Northern and Central Europe, Asia, North America—hunted, skin made into clothing.

THE WHALE.

Backboned, mammal, flesh-eater, sea-mammal—largest animal in the world, ninety to one hundred feet in length; head very large, mouth wide, has whalebone instead of teeth, soft spongy tongue, small throat, small eyes, fins under eyes, smooth skin, blubber—not a fish, must come to surface of water to breathe; fond of young—feeds by swimming with mouth open, on crabs, shrimps, sea insects—seas of cold and temperate regions—whalebone, blubber, flesh.

THE RATTLESNAKE.

Backboned, reptile, snake—five to eight feet in length, has expanding jaws, teeth contain poison, tail makes rattling sound—basks in sun, is easily subdued by music, only attacks when molested, its bite causes death—eats small animals, birds, worms, squirrels—North America.

THE EAGLE.

Backboned, bird, bird of prey—wings seven feet across, and contain strong muscles; short, sharp, hooked beak; short, strong feet; very strong, sharp claws; long tail, keen vision—solitary, builds nest on high rock or mountain side, long-lived, flies rapidly, lays two or three eggs, young called eaglets—eats birds, hares, rabbits—temperate and cold regions—feathers used for ornaments.

THE FROG.

Backboned, amphibious, frog—slight form, four legs, no tail, feet webbed, head flat, mouth large, has one row of teeth in upper jaw, large eyes, hind legs longer than fore legs—frequents ponds and ditches, moves by leaping, able to swim, torpid in winter—feeds on worms, slugs, insects, &c.—found almost in all parts of the world—destroys slugs, eaten in France and Germany.

THE ANT.

Jointed, insect, bee-tribe—small, very strong, head triangular, jaws strong, is very active, some have stings—very social, industrious, courageous; divided into males, females, and neuters; neuters are workers and soldiers; torpid in winter—found in various parts of the world—vegetable and animal food—used as food in Brazil.

ADDITIONAL SUBJECTS :—

Monkey.	Hawk.	Salmon.	Serpent.
Bat.	Owl.	Herring.	Viper.
Mole.	Crow.	Flying-fish.	Lizard.
Bear.	Parrot.	Shark.	Tortoise.
Tiger.	Cuckoo.	Sturgeon.	Beetle.
Beaver.	Turkey.	Skate.	Grasshopper
Elephant.	Pheasant.	Sword-fish.	Bee.
Seal.	Flamingo.	Trout.	Wasp.
Sloth.	Stork.	Perch.	Butterfly.
Kangaroo.	Goose.	Dog-fish.	Fly.

NATURAL HISTORY.

CHAPTER II.

NOTES OF LESSONS ON PLANTS.

AFTER animals, Plants are the natural objects with which children are most familiar, and in which they may be most easily interested. They may be used even more readily than animals as objects on which children may practically exercise their powers of observation and comparison. In dealing with a plant,—a tree, a shrub, a flower, anything belonging to the Vegetable kingdom,—the heads most suitable for arranging the matter are the following :—

       I. CLASS.
      II. DESCRIPTION.
     III. CULTIVATION.
     IV. LOCALITY.
      V. USES.
     VI. HISTORY.

I. **Class.**—Here the object is to describe generally the group to which the particular plant belongs. A popular description will generally suffice, such as that of the Mahogany tree, and the Oak as *Industrial plants*, and of the Tea plant and the Potato as *Food plants*. (See tables, pp. 22, 23.) In schools in which botany is taught systematically, the scientific classification may be used. In that case the mahogany tree will be described as belonging to the order *Cedar trees*, of the class *Exogenous plants*.

II. **Description.**—This head answers the question, What is the general appearance of the plant—what is it like? It mentions its height and size; describes its trunk, foliage, flower, bark, and seed, and the character of its growth. The Model Lesson on the Mahogany tree will show how this may be best done. The "method" under this head is very important. It consists chiefly in comparison, for the purpose of bringing out both similarity and contrast.

III. **Cultivation.**—This head tells whether the plant grows wild or is artificially cultivated. All forest trees, and all plants that grow without the tendance of man, are said to grow wild. That is what is meant by "natural growth" in the Model Lesson, though there is a sense in which all growth is natural, —is the result, that is to say, of the spontaneous working of the organs of vegetable life. The test is, Does the plant come to maturity with or without the help of man?

IV. **Locality.**—The places of which the tree is a native, or where it is chiefly cultivated, are mentioned under this head.

V. **Uses.**—This head is generally the most important in the case of a plant. It is necessary to mention, not only the uses to which it is applied, but also the mode of converting it from its natural state to that in which it becomes useful. Thus of the Mahogany tree it is stated, that after being cut down it is trimmed and cut into logs, which are drawn to the river-side by oxen, along tracks made by the traffic; that these logs are floated down the rivers to the sea in rafts, and are there shipped to England. This explains the process of bringing the tree to the timber market. The subsequent stages are dealt with in a separate paragraph—its use by cabinet-makers both in the solid form and in that of veneer. The case of the Oak, in the Comparative table, shows an interesting variety, as different parts and products of the tree are applied to different uses. In the case of the Tea plant, the leaf is the useful part; in the case of the Potato, the tubers of the root.

VI. **History.**—Give an account, under this head, of the discovery of the plant, and mention any interesting facts that may be known regarding its application to special purposes and its introduction into particular countries.

MODEL LESSON: THE MAHOGANY TREE.

Articles required.—*A piece of Mahogany Furniture—Picture of Mahogany Tree—Map of America.*

INTRODUCTION.—Refer to furniture, and the kinds of wood of which it is made.

HEADS.	MATTER.	METHOD.
CLASS.	Industrial plant.	Compare with oak, beech, or other well-known tree.
DESCRIPTION	Height.—80 to 100 feet	Compare with some tree, spire, or tower in neighbourhood.
	Trunk.—Large and solid	Compare with oak.
	Foliage.—Thick—beautiful in appearance	Compare with chestnut.
	Flowers.—Whitish or yellow...	Compare with chestnut.
	Bark.—Bitter taste—pleasant smell	Compare with Peruvian bark.
	Seed.—Winged.	Compare with thistle seed.
	Growth.—Very slow	Compare with oak (slow), sycamore (quick).
CULTIVATION	Natural growth in warm climates.	Compare with forest tree and fruit tree.
LOCALITY.	Cuba and St. Domingo (West Indies), Honduras (Central America).	Show places on map.
USES.	Cut down in April and May—branches lopped off—divided into logs—drawn to river side by oxen—floated to the sea in rafts—shipped to England. Sold to cabinet-makers—used for the best articles of furniture—cut into thin pieces and used as a covering to other woods—one log sometimes worth £1000.	Explain: no roads and no railways in these countries. Ask for names of articles made of mahogany, and explain veneering fully.
HISTORY.	Introduced into England by accident. Mahogany having been used to repair one of Sir Walter Ralegh's ships when at Trinidad, one of the British West India Islands, attention was called to the wood on his arrival at home. Gradually it advanced in public estimation, and it is now regarded as superior to any other kind for furniture-making.	Tell who Sir Walter Ralegh was, and say something about his voyages and his death.

NOTES OF LESSONS ON PLANTS. 23

COMPARISON OF PLANTS.

Arrangement of Lesson.	OAK.	TEA PLANT.	POTATO.
CLASS.	Industrial plant.	Food plant.	Food plant.
DESCRIPTION.	Height—trunk—branches—bark—leaves—fruit—gall.	Size—leaves—blossoms.	Root—stem—leaves—flower—apple.
CULTIVATION.	Natural growth—large forests—deep soil.	Stony soil—mountain slope—sowing—watering—gathering.	Sandy soil—planting—hoeing—gathering.
LOCALITY.	Hot and temperate regions—chiefly Europe and N. America.	China, Japan, and Assam.	All civilized countries.
USES.	Timber.—Ship-building—millwork—barrel staves—furniture—beams, &c. Bark.—Tanning—medicine, as a tonic—corks, from bark of cork oak. Acorns.—Food for swine—oil. Gall Nuts.—Ink—tanning—dyes.	Food.—Each leaf picked separately by a person with gloved hands—exposed to the air for a few hours—roasted and rolled—when infused, a stimulating drink is procured—the different kinds of tea are the results of different modes of preparing the leaf.	Food.—Contains a large quantity of starch—forms a nourishing vegetable.
HISTORY.	Regarded as a sacred tree by the Greeks, Romans, and ancient Britons.	Introduced into England in the sixteenth century—very dear at first—sold at £5 to £10 per pound—150,000,000 lbs. imported for home consumption in 1876.	Introduced into England from Virginia by Sir Walter Ralegh in the reign of Queen Elizabeth—though not well received at first, it soon became the chief vegetable used.

EXERCISES.

Matter for Notes of Lessons to be arranged on the plan of the Model Lesson.

THE DAISY.

A wild flower—white petals tipped with crimson or red and arranged like a star; yellow heart; flower held in green cup; short wiry stalk; thick green leaves—grows in the fields and by the wayside; found low down in the grass; in bloom all the year; opens when the sun shines; closes at night—makes the fields look pretty; children gather daisies to make into chains.

THE ELM.

An industrial plant—lofty and graceful; large trunk; thick foliage; rough dark green leaves; smooth bark on branches; rugged trunk; dark red flowers; oval green pod; one seed—often planted in rows along carriage-drives and in parks—very common in England and in all temperate climates—wood hard and tough; used for water-wheels, embankments, bottoms of ships, building, carving, &c.

THE SUGAR CANE.

A food plant—from 15 to 20 feet in height; bright yellow leaves; lilac blossoms—propagated from cuttings or shoots; planted horizontally; a new stalk springs from each joint—cut close to ground when ripe—tropical countries; India, China, West Indies, South America—crushed between heavy rollers; the juice is manufactured into sugar—sugar and molasses, or treacle, are articles of food; tops are used as fodder for cattle—its introduction into Europe was one of the results of the Crusades.

THE BIRCH.

An industrial plant—beautiful in appearance; small light green leaves; elegant drooping boughs; silver-white bark—grows on the bleak mountain-side; seems to prefer exposed situations—colder regions of Europe and Asia; the only tree in Greenland—the bark more durable than the wood; made into boats; used to thatch houses, for clothing, ground with corn as food, yields oil, used for tanning leather: dye prepared from leaves: wood makes good charcoal for gunpowder, used for smoking hams and fish, and for general purposes—the bundles of rods carried before Roman magistrates were made of birch twigs.

THE PRIMROSE.

A wild flower—pale yellow colour; five petals; tubular green calyx; naked stem; soft green leaves; sweet perfume—grows in woods, on banks, by the water-side, blooms in spring—found in Europe and north of Asia—cultivated as garden flower and window plant.

THE COFFEE TREE.

A food plant—about 9 feet high; slender branches; evergreen leaves; white blossoms; red berry; oval seeds—grown on the slopes of hills; well watered and weeded; berries gathered in May—West Indies, Central and South America, Arabia, Ceylon; wild in Abyssinia—dried by sun; husk broken by stone rollers; berries roasted and ground; made into an agreeable drink—coffee-houses first established in London about 1652.

THE COMMON ORANGE.

A fruit—round, top and bottom flat; yellow colour; thick rind; sweet juice, soft pulp—rich soil; strong clay; open air in warm climates, green-houses in cold climates—south of Europe, China—used for food; cooling and refreshing; oil from rind—introduced into Italy by the Moors about 1400.

THE RICE PLANT.

A food plant—resembles both barley and oats; grain grows on separate stalks springing from main stalk—only in hot countries, and on marshy soil; ground often flooded; much weeding; two harvests in a year; cut down with sickle—India, China, America, Egypt—husk removed; made into bread, puddings, starch; straw made into bonnets and hats; chief dish for all ranks in the East.

ADDITIONAL SUBJECTS :—

Ash.	Pear.	Rose.	Arrowroot.
Box.	Cherry.	Pansy.	Bamboo.
Sycamore.	Plum.	Lily.	Cinnamon.
Beech.	Cocoa-nut.	Poppy.	Palm.
Poplar.	Grape.	Snowdrop.	Tobacco plant.
Chestnut.	Fig.	Foxglove.	Cork tree.
Holly.	Pea.	Buttercup.	Cotton plant.

NATURAL HISTORY.

CHAPTER III.

NOTES OF LESSONS ON MINERALS.

THE heads under which a Mineral is treated do not differ greatly from those used in dealing with animals and plants. The following will be found sufficiently detailed :—

    I. CLASS.
    II. DESCRIPTION.
    III. QUALITIES.
    IV. PRODUCTION.
    V. LOCALITY.
    VI. USES.

I. **Class.**—It is not difficult to recognize the difference between metal and rock or stone—classes which suggest the most general division of the Mineral kingdom. When we go beyond this, a mineral may be classified either popularly, according to the use made of it, or scientifically, according to its structure and geological history. For the purposes of elementary teaching, the former is preferable; and that is the classification employed in the following outlines. Thus, iron is defined as the chief industrial metal—that is, the metal most largely used in the industrial arts; gold as a precious metal; the diamond as a precious stone.

II. **Description.**—The general aspect of the mineral is all that need be entered under this head. Thus we say of iron that it is of a blackish gray colour in its crude state, and that its surface is very bright when polished; of gold, we say that it is of a bright yellow colour; of marble, that it is of various colours, and very beautiful when polished; of coal, that it is black, glistening, and stone-like, and that it is of vegetable origin.

III. **Qualities.**—This is the most important head, in the case of minerals, because it includes all those things which characterize a particular mineral and distinguish it from others. It should always be noted that it is not any one quality that gives a mineral its character, but the sum of all its qualities. Both iron and gold are malleable, ductile, fusible, heavy, and sonorous; yet there are great differences between them, apart from the rarity of the one and the abundance of the other. Iron is applied to many purposes for which gold would be useless, even if it could be obtained in sufficient quantity. Gold would be of little use, for example, in making a steam-engine or a bridge. Again, both iron and marble are hard, while both iron and coal are brittle, though in different degrees. Thus it appears that it is not enough to mention that a mineral possesses this or that quality; all the qualities which distinguish it from other minerals must be stated. It is essential, too, that the words used to describe the qualities be explained, and that the qualities themselves be illustrated by familiar comparisons and contrasts.

IV. **Production.**—It is the purpose of this head to explain how the mineral is obtained in its natural state, and the processes by which it is prepared for use. Thus, in the lesson on Iron, mention is made not only of the manner in which the metal is found, but also of the processes through which it passes, and of the forms which it ultimately assumes. In the Comparative table, the two forms in which gold is found are stated,—in "nuggets" and in grains; and the difference between marble *quarries* and coal *mines* is obvious and instructive.

V. and VI. **Locality: Uses.**—These heads include the same kinds of particulars as the same heads in the case of plants and animals. The uses to which minerals are applied are very numerous and varied, and their elucidation affords excellent material for useful lessons.

MODEL LESSON: IRON.

Articles required.—*Iron Ore—Nail—Scissors—Map of Europe.*
INTRODUCTION.—Show Nail, ask what it is made of, then get description and qualities of the material.

HEADS.	MATTER.	METHOD.
CLASS.	Chief industrial metal.	Compare with gold. Contrast with stone.
DESCRIPTION	A fibrous metal—blackish-gray colour—found mixed with other minerals—when polished, very bright.	Show iron ore; also unpolished and polished iron.
QUALITIES.	**Elastic.**—The most elastic of metals, when made into steel.	Illustrate by springs.
	Ductile.—May be drawn into wire..............	Explain, wire as fine as human hair.
	Heavy.—Between seven and eight times heavier than water..............	Show that one cubic inch of iron weighs as much as seven of water.
	Brittle.—Easily broken	Compare with glass. Contrast with lead.
	Hard.—Especially as steel	Illustrate by blacksmith's anvil.
	Malleable.—May be beaten out.	Ask for articles made of wrought iron.
	Sonorous.—Loud sounding....	Illustrate by bells.
	Fusible.—Melts when subjected to great heat......	Explain action of furnace.
PRODUCTION.	Dug out of mines—ore crushed—placed in furnace—iron separated from dross—then it is *cast iron*—heated again and worked it becomes *wrought iron*—heated again by charcoal, it becomes *steel*.	Compare ore, dross, iron, wrought iron, steel. Explain that wrought iron is cast iron freed from carbon and beaten and rolled.
LOCALITY.	The commonest of metals—found in every country—Great Britain, Sweden, Belgium, and France are noted for their iron mines.	Show these countries on map.
	Of most value when found with coal.	Explain that coal is needed to work iron.
USES.	The most useful of metals—used in almost every trade. Newcastle makes machinery—Sheffield makes cutlery—Birmingham, in the "Black Country," makes everything that can be made of iron, from a nail to a steam-engine.	Ask for names of articles made of iron, as weapons, machines, tools, bridges, parts of buildings, &c. Give a description of the "Black Country" by day and by night. Explain why so called.

NOTES OF LESSONS ON MINERALS.

COMPARISON OF MINERALS.

Arrangement of Lesson.	GOLD.	MARBLE.	COAL.
INTRODUCTION	Refer to coins—Show a gold coin.	Show a stone—Ask for names of finer kinds of stone.	Refer to fire—Show a piece of coal.
CLASS.	A precious metal.	A fine kind of limestone.	An inflammable fossil.
DESCRIPTION.	Bright yellow colour — found mixed with other minerals.	Of various colours—very beautiful when polished.	Black, glistening, stone-like mineral, of vegetable origin.
QUALITIES.	A perfect metal — malleable — ductile — heavy — fusible — pliable—compact—sonorous.	Hard — close-grained — sparkling—"saccharine" (loafsugar-like).	Black—brittle.
PRODUCTION.	Found in "nuggets" and in grains—in quartz, in beds of rivers, and in alluvial deposits—separated from the dross by crushing the ore with heavy machines.	Found in mountains—cut out in large blocks, from openings called quarries.	Dug out of mines—miners are exposed to great dangers—sometimes explosions take place or water bursts into the mines, and many lives are lost.
LOCALITY.	Gold mines Brazil, Peru, Mexico—diggings California, Australia—gold mixed with sand, American and African rivers.	Italian marble is best—the Appennines contains nearly every variety—famous quarries exist at Carrara.	Britain is famous for its coal-fields—the Newcastle coal-field is the largest in the world.
USES.	The most precious of all metals—coins—ornaments—gilding.	The finest of all stones—used by carvers and sculptors for ornamental stones and statues.	Fuel for fires—for engines—for furnaces—used in making gas—40 million tons are raised yearly.

EXERCISES.

Matter for Notes of Lessons to be arranged on the plan of the Model Lesson.

SILVER.

A precious metal—white and shining, found in a pure state and also as an ore—a perfect metal, malleable, ductile, heavy, fusible, soft, reflective, compact, sweetly sonorous—dug out of mines, ore crushed, separated from other substances by means of mercury, melted in a furnace, and made into ingots—America, Asia, various parts of Europe, small quantities in English lead mines—coins, spoons, forks, various articles used at the table, ornaments, watches, plated goods.

SALT.

A mineral used in food—white saline substance found in rocks—sparkling, crystalline, soluble, fusible, brittle—*sea salt* or bay salt is produced from the ocean, *rock salt* is dug out of the earth—chief English mine in Cheshire, the most remarkable near Cracow in Poland—used in food, for preserving or curing meat, fish, &c., in various manufactures.

CLAY.

A dull, earthy mineral, of various colours—when moist, it is soft, plastic, easily polished; when dry, it is hard, porous, absorbent—dug out of beds, where it is found in large quantities—common in all parts of the Earth—earthenware is made of the purer kinds; bricks, flower-pots, chimney-pots, &c., are made of the coarser kinds.

THE DIAMOND.

A precious stone—usually colourless like water, sometimes white, gray, yellow, green, &c.—very valuable, the hardest of all known substances, very brilliant, transparent, combustible—diamond mines are generally only diggings or washings of alluvial deposits; slaves are employed in diamond washing—India, Brazil, Ural mountains—as ornaments; in cutting and polishing all kinds of gems; in watchmaking; in artificial teeth making; by glaziers—famous diamonds: the Koh-i-noor, the Orlow diamond, the Pitt diamond, the Sancy diamond.

CHALK.

A soft kind of limestone—white, dull-looking mineral—friable, yielding, infusible—dug from pits, cut out of the sides of hills—abundant in England, large quantities in the neighbourhood of London, chalk hills on the south-east of England—made into mortar and whiting; used for writing on slates, black-boards, &c.

SLATE.

An industrial clay—dark gray mineral substance, easily divided into thin layers—dull, compact, brittle, soft—obtained from quarries, detached by crowbars or blasting, split by wedges, &c.—abundant in Wales, west of England, parts of Scotland and Ireland; about 2,000 men and boys are employed at the celebrated Penrhyn quarries near Bangor—for roofing houses; for writing on; for paving; for cisterns, baths, pencils, &c.

ADDITIONAL SUBJECTS:—

Tin.	Limestone.	Fuller's-earth.
Copper.	Gypsum.	Alum.
Lead.	Flint.	Emery.
Zinc.	Sandstone.	Pumicestone.
Mercury.	Mica.	Sulphur.

MANUFACTURES.

CHAPTER IV.

NOTES OF LESSONS ON MANUFACTURED ARTICLES.

LESSONS on Manufactured Articles are among the most interesting and useful that can be given in elementary schools. Both their interest and their utility depend on the "matter" being clearly laid out. Careful "method" is also indispensable here, because it is always difficult to make children follow with interest the steps in a process which they may never have seen. In this connection, pictures and diagrams are of great use. The heads to be adopted in arranging the matter are these:—

   I. DESCRIPTION.
   II. QUALITIES.
   III. MATERIAL.
   IV. PROCESS OF MANUFACTURE.
   V. USES.
   VI. HISTORY.

The only head that differs from those in previous chapters, and that requires special remark, is the fourth,—**Process of Manufacture.** Under this head the several steps of the process must be arranged in the order in which they occur, and must be carefully described. Thus, in the Model Lesson on Coins (p. 33), each step in the process of manufacture forms a separate sub-head, not only as regards the matter, but also as regards the method.

It will be noticed that such motive powers as Steam and Electricity, though not "manufactured articles" in the ordinary sense, are yet capable of the same treatment.

NOTES OF LESSONS ON MANUFACTURED ARTICLES. 33

MODEL LESSON: ENGLISH COINS.

Articles required.—*Several coins—Thimble—Piece of clay.*

INTRODUCTION.—Ask what we must take to a shop in order to obtain any article we may require from it—Ask what money consists of.

HEADS.	MATTER.	METHOD.
DESCRIPTION	Stamped metal used for money.	Show convenience of this; contrast with barter.
QUALITIES.	Round — flat — bright — hard — durable—valuable.	Illustrate qualities by giving or asking for other examples of them
MATERIAL.	Gold—silver—bronze.	Ask for examples.
PROCESS OF MANUFACTURE.	**Preparation of Metal.**—Gold and silver have copper mixed with them. Bronze is a mixture of copper and tin....	Explain that this is done to secure hardness and durability, these metals in a pure state being too soft to bear the wear and tear the coinage is subject to.
	Rolled.—Passed between heavy rollers..............	To produce the proper thickness.
	Punched.—Pieces cut the size of a coin, and called "blanks"	Illustrate by thimble and piece of clay.
	Weighed.—In self-acting balance, which rejects light and heavy "blanks."	Show importance of weight and sound as tests of good and bad coins.
	Sounded.—Rung on a sounding iron..............	
	Milled.—Fine grooves made round the edges	Explain: to prevent coin being clipped.
	Stamped.—With the monarch's likeness, name, date, &c. ..	Show that this makes it a legal coin.
USES.	Given in exchange for goods and as payment for work—twelve in number:— **Gold.**—Sovereign and half-sovereign. **Silver.**— Crown, half-crown, florin, shilling, sixpence, fourpence, threepence. **Bronze.**— Penny, halfpenny, farthing	Show the necessity for coins having a real value as metal. Illustrate by shells, beads, &c., being used in uncivilized countries.
HISTORY.	The first English coin was a silver penny. This penny was marked with a cross, by which it could be broken into four pieces, called fourth-things or farthings. When shillings were first made, twenty were made out of one pound of silver.	Show that the use of coins became a necessity as man's wants increased, and as he became more civilized.

3

COMPARISON OF MANUFACTURED ARTICLES.

Arrangement of Lesson.	GLASS.	PAPER.	A STEEL PEN.
INTRODUCTION	*Refer to a window, &c.*	*Refer to a book, &c.*	*Refer to writing materials.*
DESCRIPTION.	A substance used in making windows, bottles, tumblers, &c.	The material of which books are made.	An instrument for writing.
QUALITIES.	Bright — smooth — hard — transparent — brittle.	Flexible — smooth — stiff — easily torn.	Bright — hard — elastic.
MATERIALS.	Sand — alkali — lime.	Linen rags — straw, &c.	Steel — from Swedish iron.
PROCESS OF MANUFACTURE	Materials are mixed — put into a furnace — heated — placed in a second furnace — rolled out — blown — heated again — cooled gradually — manufactured at St. Helens, Newcastle, Birmingham, Edinburgh, &c.	Rags picked and sorted — reduced to pulp — strained — passed over wire-cloth — pressed between rollers — sized — pressed.	Steel is cut into sheets — cleansed — rolled — cut into strips — pieces punched out — pierced — stamped — raised — hardened — tempered — scoured — slit — coloured and varnished. Made at Birmingham.
USES.	Flint glass is used for telescopes — plate and crown, for windows — common, for bottles.	For writing — printing — packing — for making papier-maché goods, &c.	For writing on paper or other material with a fluid called ink.
HISTORY.	Mica was used for windows before the invention of glass, which was said to have been the result of an accident.	The inner bark of trees, papyrus, skins of animals (called parchment), and tables of wax were used in ancient times as substitutes for paper.	In ancient times a reed was used — pens were at first made of quills — steel pens have been in use about 100 years.

EXERCISES.

Matter for Notes of Lessons to be arranged on the plan of the Model Lesson.

A NEEDLE.

A small instrument used for sewing—bright, tapering, pointed, fusible, hard, brittle, solid—steel wire—wire cut into lengths; heated, straightened, pointed, stamped, pierced, cut, hardened, tempered, polished, turned, finished; passes through the hands of one hundred and twenty workmen—the chief seat of manufacture, Redditch in Worcestershire; sewing—introduced into England in the reign of Queen Mary; called at first "a domestic treasure;" fish bones and thorns used before needles were invented.

LEATHER.

The material of which boots and shoes are made—flexible, waterproof, odorous, tough, durable—skins of animals: sheep, lambs, deer, dogs, seals, hogs, &c.—the skin is scraped, soaked, cleansed, tanned, dried, rolled, curried, blackened—for shoes, gloves, saddles, reins, covers of books, portmanteaus.

BREAD.

Food made of ground grain—wholesome, nutritious, edible, soft—flour, various kinds of crushed grain—salt, yeast, water—materials mixed and made into dough; leavened; baked in an oven—food—wheaten bread once regarded as a luxury where it is now very common; barley, oats, and rye chiefly used in former times.

WOOLLEN CLOTH.

Wool woven into a piece—soft, flexible, tough, durable, dry—short-fibred fine wool cut from the sheep—the wool is sorted, washed, dyed, carded, spun, woven, felted, pressed—chief manufactories at Leeds, Halifax, Huddersfield, &c.—wool was at first imported from Germany and other parts of the Continent, now it is chiefly imported from Australia and Cape Colony.

OIL.

A greasy fluid—semi-transparent, liquid, penetrating, thick, light, inflammable, odorous—animal; from whales, seals, &c. : vegetable; from the olive, the palm, the flax plant, coleseed, &c. : mineral; from bitumen—obtained by subjecting the animal or vegetable substance to great pressure or to heat; mineral oil is obtained by distillation—food, medicine, paint-making, lamps, &c.

A BELL.

A hollow body of metal, which makes a noise when struck—hard, heavy, concave, sonorous—bell-metal (a mixture of copper and tin), also brass, silver, gold—metal melted, poured into mould, left to cool, trimmed, tongue fixed—placed in church steeples; fixed to buoys on sunken rocks, &c.; gives notice to work-people; attached to clocks; used in houses, &c.—of ancient origin; mentioned in the Bible; used by the Greeks and the Romans: first used in churches about 400 A.D.: largest bell in the world at Moscow; it weighs one hundred and twenty-three tons.

GLUE.

A sticky animal substance—hard, bright, brown, solid, artificial; when melted, tough, adhesive, tenacious—horns, hoofs, sinews of various animals, scrapings and cuttings of skins—cleansed, boiled, strained, boiled again, poured out in layers, cut into squares, dried—for sticking parts of furniture, &c., together.

STEAM.

Water made into vapour by great heat—elastic, very powerful, invisible (when cooling, like mist)—water and heat—water is placed in a vessel over a fire; when the water boils it passes off as steam—steam is confined in a boiler; in trying to escape, the steam works the engine—known for three hundred years as a moving power: Watt improved the steam engine; Stephenson made the first railway engine.

ADDITIONAL SUBJECTS:—

Sugar.	Linen.	Candle.	Pin.
Coffee.	Silk.	Soap.	Book.
Butter.	Velvet.	Gas.	Thimble.
Cheese.	Cotton.	Scissors.	Cup.

READING.

CHAPTER V.

NOTES OF LESSONS ON READING.

THE chief object in giving a Reading Lesson is to secure good reading. But we read for information; we read aloud to impart information; and that is the best reading which best conveys to the mind the sense intended, not that which makes the most pleasant sound. Now a reader cannot convey sense which he has not himself grasped; and therefore it is essential to good reading that the reader shall first clearly understand that which is to be read.

The first thing to be done, therefore, in giving a reading lesson, is to explain difficulties—to remove hindrances to the clear comprehension of the meaning of what is to be read. These difficulties may consist in words not previously met with by the class, and may relate both to pronunciation and to meaning. They may consist in historical and literary allusions, or in the nature of the subject-matter itself. The treatment will differ with the state of advancement of the class; and also with the character of the subject, especially according as it may be a passage of prose or a passage of poetry. The Notes of a Lesson on a passage of Prose (for an elementary class) may therefore be arranged under the following heads:—

      I. EXAMPLE.
     II. SUBJECT-MATTER.
    III. PRONUNCIATION.
    IV. MEANINGS.
     V. ELOCUTION.

I. **Example.**—This is the passage which is to be read.

II. **Subject-Matter.**—Under this head a brief summary of the chief points in the lesson is given. It is, in fact, an object-lesson in a condensed form.

III. **Pronunciation.**—Under this head words of difficult or peculiar pronunciation are noted. The teacher should write such words on the black-board, in syllables and with accents.

IV. **Meanings.**—This head contains explanations of difficult words and phrases.

V. **Elocution.**—Under this head attention is called to those qualities which make reading effective. They are,—

1. **Expression.**—This means throwing proper feeling into the reading of the passage, according as it is pathetic, cheerful, humorous, or heroic.

2. **Inflection.**—This relates to the rising and falling of the voice. The proper use of the rising and the falling inflection prevents reading from being monotonous.

3. **Emphasis.**—This is the stress laid on particular words, for the purpose of calling attention to them. Contrasted words and ideas are in this way brought into prominence.

4. **Pause.**—There must often be a pause where there is no punctuation mark. Sometimes it serves to arrest the attention at a particular word or point in the sentence. Sometimes it is used for the purpose of showing what words are to be separated, and what words are to be connected, in meaning.

The Notes of a Lesson on a passage of Poetry (for an advanced class) will include matters of greater difficulty, and should be arranged under these heads :—

    I. EXAMPLE.
    II. CIRCUMSTANCES.
    III. SUBJECT-MATTER.
    IV. CONSTRUCTION.
    V. EXPLANATION.
    VI. ELOCUTION.

I. **Example.**—This is the prescribed passage, as before. The teacher should mention from what work the passage is taken, and the connection in which it stands. Thus, in the Model Lesson (p. 41), it is stated that the passage is taken from Shakespeare's play of *King John*, and is spoken by Prince Arthur, after Hubert had told him that his eyes were to be burned out with red-hot irons.

II. **Circumstances.**—The object of this head is to bring the scene described, or in which the words are supposed to be spoken, vividly before the class. On this the effective reading of the passage in great measure depends.

III. **Subject-Matter.**—This head tells in a few words the general drift of the passage.

IV. **Construction.**—This head is the most important of the whole. Its object is to fill up ellipses, and to explain peculiar grammatical constructions. The passage cannot be understood, and therefore cannot be intelligently read, until this shall have been done.

V. **Explanation.**—Difficult words and allusions are explained under this head. In the Model Lesson, "iron age" refers to the division of early times into gold, silver, bronze, and iron ages. But there is in the expression also a play on the word "irons" used by Hubert, as well as a reference to the hard and cruel nature of King John. All such points as would form the subjects of notes in an annotated edition of the poem belong to this head.

VI. **Elocution.**—This includes, as in the former case, notes on expression, inflection, emphasis, and pause.

After the passage has been carefully examined as to its meaning, and when all difficulties have been removed, it should be taken up as an exercise in Elocution. The common custom of requiring the class to read the passage before it is critically examined is wrong in principle and injurious in practice. Mistakes made in a first reading are not easily got rid of afterwards.

MODEL LESSON: PROSE READING. (Standard III.)

INTRODUCTION.—Refer to flight of swallows, and to swallow's nest.

HEADS.	MATTER.	METHOD.
EXAMPLE.	"There are *some* ' birds which do not live in England all the year round. ' When *winter* comes ' they fly away to *warmer* ' lands, and return again in *spring*. The *swallow* is one of these birds. ' It spends the winter in *Africa*, ' and does not come back to *England* until the month of *March* or April. Few birds fly so fast ' as swallows. Their speed is said to be more than a mile ' a minute, or greater ' than that of the fastest railway train. They *never* seem to tire, but dart ' about, now here ' and now ' there, after the insects ' on which they feed."— *Royal Reader* (2nd Series) No. III., page 90.	Explain that this is part of a lesson on the swallow. Describe the bird—its long, pointed wings—its short feet—its wide mouth, adapted for catching insects in the air—its swift flight—its clumsy gait when on its feet—its shrill cry.
SUBJECT-MATTER.	1. Swallows are "birds of passage." 2. They spend the summer in England, and the winter in Africa. 3. They return to England in March or April. 4. They fly very quickly. 5. They feed on insects.	1. Refer to other birds of passage,—cuckoo, nightingale. 2. Show "England" and "Africa" on the map; and show that Africa is crossed by the Equator, while England is far from it. 3. The weather then begins to be mild. 4. Compare with rate of railway train. 5. Few insects in the air in cold weather.
PRONUNCIATION.	"England," pronounced Ing´-gland. "Swallow," pronounced swaw´-lo.	Be careful to insist on distinct articulation.
MEANINGS.	"All the year round," through all seasons; always. "Warmer lands," countries farther south. "Return," come back.	Require the phrases to be varied by substituting others of like meaning.
ELOCUTION.	Expression: light and cheerful. Inflection: rising, at words marked '. Emphasis: on words printed in italics.	Read the passage slowly; and then require it to be read by the class, singly and collectively.

MODEL LESSON: POETICAL READING.

INTRODUCTION.—Refer to the play (King John) from which the passage is taken, and specially to Prince Arthur's part in it.

HEADS.	MATTER.	METHOD.
EXAMPLE.	*Arth.* "Ah, none but in this iron age would do it! The iron of itself, though heat red-hot, Approaching near these eyes, would drink my And quench his fiery indignation [tears, Even in the matter of mine innocence: Nay, after that, consume away in rust, But for containing fire to harm mine eye. Are you more stubborn-hard than hammered iron? An if an *angel* should have come to me, And told me *Hubert* should put out mine eyes, I would not have believed him,—no tongue but *Hubert's*."	Explain that the words are spoken by Prince Arthur, in reply to Hubert, the King's chamberlain, who has told him that he has been ordered to burn out his eyes with red-hot irons.
CIRCUM-STANCES.	A dismal room inside a prison—a timid boy standing before a powerful man.	Scene must be vividly realized
SUBJECT-MATTER.	Arthur tries to coax Hubert from his cruel purpose.	Explain the drift of the passage.
CONSTRUC-TION.	"Ah, none but *those who live* in this iron age would do it (*would burn out mine eyes*). The iron of itself, though *heated* red-hot, approaching (*when it approached*) near these eyes, would drink my tears, and quench his fiery indignation even in the matter of mine innocence: nay, after that, *the iron would* consume away in rust, but for containing (*only because it contained*) fire to harm mine eye. Are you more stubborn-hard than hammered iron? An if an angel should have come to me, and *should have* told me *that* Hubert should put out mine eyes, I would not have believed him,—*I would believe* no tongue but Hubert's *own*."	Fill up all ellipses, and explain or paraphrase all peculiar grammatical constructions. The passage cannot be intelligently read until this shall have been done.
EXPLANA-TION.	Line 1. "Iron age"—a reference to the ancient division of early times into gold, silver, bronze, and iron ages. 4. "Fiery indignation," refers to the hissing of red-hot iron when it touches water. 5. "The matter of mine innocence"—my tears.	Explain the play on the word "irons" used by Hubert, and the reference to the cruel nature of King John.
ELOCUTION.	Expression: playfully sad. Inflection: mostly the rising. Emphasis: on italic words.	Read the passage to the class as it should be read.

WRITING.

CHAPTER VI.

NOTES OF LESSONS ON WRITING.

TILL lately, there was no common subject in the school course on which so little care and system were bestowed as on Writing. In many schools writing was not taught, it was simply practised. The writing lesson was considered a convenient device for keeping one class quietly occupied while the teacher was taking another class in reading or in arithmetic. The children went on filling the pages of their copy-books, with hardly any supervision or correction. The consequence was that they went on repeating their old mistakes and adding new ones, line after line, and page after page. It is true that the state of matters in this respect has improved greatly during recent years, but that there is still great room for improvement is evident from the Reports of H. M. Inspectors.

Good results in writing can be obtained only by each exercise in writing being made the subject of a special and systematic lesson. The following Model Lesson is intended to show how this may be done. It is not the object of these Notes to show how a complete course of lessons in writing should be arranged. Their object is simply to show how a writing lesson should be given to a particular class, and at the same time how the Notes of any such lesson may be drawn up.

There is, however, a preliminary point that must be settled, namely, on what method the writing lesson should be given. There are two methods of teaching writing,—the Analytic and the Imitative. The Analytic method is that which treats all the letters as combinations of certain common elements; which presents the letters to the child in the order of their increasing complexity; and which holds that the slope, the length, and the spacing of the letters, depend on ascertained rules.* The Imitative method puts a good model—a complete word or a short sentence—before the scholar, and instructs him to copy it as closely as he can. That imitation must always play an important part in learning to write is undeniable. But to rely on imitation alone in the teaching of writing is not wise; because, when a mistake is made, that method does not enable the teacher to give any reason for its being a mistake, except that the writing does not correspond with the model. The teacher ought to be able to give some reason for the model being right and for the scholar's copy being wrong. Another reason for preferring the analytic method is, that it makes the writing lesson more interesting and more useful educationally, than the other. Further, it is the system now most generally used, and it has therefore been adopted in the following Notes.

The Notes are arranged under these heads :—

   I. EXAMPLE.
   II. DETAILS.
   III. DIRECTIONS.
   IV. QUALITIES.

I. **Example.**—This is the word or line that is to be written by the class,—the "copy" that forms the lesson of the day. The word "mingled" has been chosen, because it has variety both in the length of the letters and in their spacing. Whether the word be written as a head-line in the copy-books or not, it should be written on the black-board by the teacher. This is the first step in the lesson. When the word has been written on the board, the attention of the whole class should be called to it. The teacher should then go over it letter by letter, referring to the points mentioned under the next head.

II. **Details.**—This head includes the several points necessary to be attended to in forming and combining the letters.

* The Analytic method has been most fully described by Mulhäuser (pron. *Moolhoiser*), a German educationist; and after him it is sometimes called the Mulhauser system.

1. Size.—This is generally determined by the ruling of the copy-books. When this is not the case, the scholars should be directed not to make the writing very small, and to make it round and bold.

2. Slope.—Mulhäuser's rule, generally accepted, is to adopt a slope of 60°.

3. Distance.—The distances between down-strokes connected by a single hook or turn should be equal. The best distance to adopt is half the perpendicular height of the letter. When two down-strokes are connected by a double hook (for example, between *i* and *n*) the distance is increased by one-half. This also occurs after the curved letters *c*, *e*, and *o*.

4. Length.—Make *l* and the long stroke of *d* twice as long as *i*, and the loop of *g* rather more than twice as long.

5. Down-strokes.—These should be of uniform thickness, and should have smooth edges.

6. Hooks.—These must be uniform and light; the down-stroke must taper sweetly into the hook; and all the letters must be joined.

III. Directions.—When these points have been carefully gone over, the class is prepared to begin to write the word; but before they do so, and while they are writing, the teacher must see that each scholar is (1) sitting in a good position, and (2) holding his pen properly. Slovenliness in either respect will inevitably produce bad writing.

IV. Qualities.—The qualities noted under this head relate not only to a particular lesson, but to all writing. It is essential, in the first place, that writing be *legible*, or easily read. One great means of making it so is to keep it *simple*, free from ornaments; and *round*, approaching to the character of print. Wide *spacing* between one word and another in the same line makes writing easily read. Lastly, writing should be *tidy*, not only for the sake of the writing, but also for the sake of the writer. The writing lesson gives opportunities for teaching neatness, order, and good taste, such as do not occur in connection with any other part of ordinary school work.

MODEL LESSON: WRITING.

HEADS.	MATTER.	METHOD.
EXAMPLE.	*mingled*	Write the "example" on the blackboard, and call attention to each of the "details" mentioned under that head.
DETAILS.	1. **Size**: determined by ruling of copy-book. 2. **Slope**: angle of 60° generally recommended. 3. **Distances**: equal, except between *i* and *n*, *e* and *d*. 4. **Length**: *l* and *d* twice the length of *i*. 5. **Down-strokes**: uniform thickness; edges smooth. 6. **Hooks**: uniform and light: all the letters to be joined.	The black-board should be ruled with oblique lines, to show the slope. The more elementary copy-books may be ruled in part in the same way. Show that the double hook after *i* and the projecting loop of *e* cause the distance to be increased by a half space.
DIRECTIONS.	1. **Position of body**: left shoulder forward; head erect; left hand on paper. 2. **Manner of holding the pen**: with first and second fingers and thumb, all extended; third finger folded in; fourth finger resting on paper	Check any scholar who drops his head on his left shoulder, or who sprawls over the desk. Make the class hold up hands with pen in position; see that the penholder rests on third joint of first finger.
QUALITIES.	Good writing must be :— 1. **Legible**: easily read. 2. **Simple**: without flourishes or ornaments. 3. **Round**: like print letters; not angular. 4. **Spaced**: letters not too close, and words well apart. 5. **Tidy**: free from blots and corrections.	The whole class should write the same exercise at the same time, and under supervision. At the end of each line, pens should be laid down and copybooks shown up. Faults should be pointed out before the next line is begun.

ARITHMETIC.

CHAPTER VII.

NOTES OF LESSONS ON ARITHMETIC.

1. SIMPLE SUBTRACTION.

THIS lesson will be given to a very elementary class—to Standard I. The explanations must therefore be very simple, and the steps in the process must be made very plain. The Model Lesson is not intended to be the first lesson in Subtraction. The children are supposed to have been working simple sums for some time, both mentally and on their slates, but not sums involving "carrying." That process has to be explained about the stage at which the Model Lesson is supposed to be given.

It is arranged under these heads:—

    I. DEFINITION.
    II. EXAMPLES.
    III. RULE.
    IV. PROCESS.
    V. PROOF.

I. **Definition.**—Besides describing the process, this serves to explain its purpose. The point to be chiefly insisted on, and to be illustrated by examples in concrete things, is, that the object is *to find what is left*. There is a great advantage in using real objects—books, marbles, nuts, even stones picked up in the play-ground, if nothing better can be had. On no account should the children be allowed to use strokes made on their slates when counting, or to count on their fingers.

II. **Examples.** — These are simple sums, intended to be worked first mentally, and afterwards on the black-board. The object of these examples is to prepare the scholars for "carrying" by practising them in exercises in which the upper figure is greater than 9.

III. **Rule.**—This describes the operation in general terms. The process of carrying is explained under the next head.

IV. **Process.** — Under this head an easy sum involving carrying is worked out step by step. The process of carrying is shown in the "matter" column, and is described in the "method" column. The theory of the process is not explained, because at this stage children can hardly be expected to understand it, and because they can quite well use the process correctly without understanding the reason of it.

The explanation of the theory may come at a later stage. There are several ways of giving this, but the best is that which goes on the principle of equal additions. The axiom on which it depends is this :—

If equals be added to unequals, the difference will be the same.

Show on the black-board that the difference between 7 and 3 is the same as the difference between 7 + 1 and 3 + 1, or between 7 + 10 and 3 + 10. Now "carrying" in subtraction is nothing but adding 10 to each line, but in different ways. In the upper line you add 10 to the units, and in the under line you add 1 to the tens, which is the same thing; in the upper line you add 10 to the tens, and in the under line you add 1 to the hundreds, which is the same thing; and so on.

V. **Proof.**—There are, of course, two ways of "proving" a sum in subtraction;—by subtracting the answer from the upper line, when the difference should be the same as the under line; and by adding the answer to the under line, when the sum will be the same as the upper line. The latter is the more convenient and the more usual. It is also theoretically the more systematic, because it reverses the operation—proving subtraction by addition.

2. REDUCTION OF MONEY.

This is a third or fourth standard lesson, and may be used as the first lesson in the rule. The scholars are already familiar with the money table, and with the process of changing one denomination of money into the next lower or higher, from their practice in the compound rules. What they have now to learn is, how to combine several steps of change in one sum,—to convert one denomination into another farther removed than the next lower or higher.

The heads under which the lesson is arranged are the following:—

    I. DEFINITION.
    II. EXAMPLES.
    III. RULE.
    IV. PROCESS.
    V. PROOF.

I. **Definition.**—This explains the object of the process, and children will follow the process more intelligently if they know whither it tends. The important point to keep before the class is, that there is no change of value involved in the process—that the sum to be reduced, the final answer, and all the intermediate denominations, are of exactly the same value. Thus, £5 = 100 shillings = 1200 pence = 4800 farthings.

II. **Examples.**—These are to be used in the first instance as mental exercises, in order to illustrate the process, and to draw out from the class the principle or rule of working which forms the next head.

III. **Rule.**—This states the principle or rule of working in a handy form, and should be committed to memory.

IV. **Process.**—Under this head two sums are worked out,—one in the descending, and one in the ascending scale. In working these on the black-board, the explanations given in the "method" column should be used and amplified.

V. **Proof.**—This will be useful, not only as a test of accurate working, but as a new illustration of the rule.

3. THE VULGAR FRACTION.

The heads under which the lesson is arranged are these :—

     I. Definition.
     II. Examples.
     III. Parts.
     IV. Kinds.
     V. Application.

I. Definition.—In dealing with this, "method" must be taken first. The illustration must precede the definition in words. Illustrations of various kinds may be used. The unit may be represented by a line or a square drawn on the black-board, or by a cake or an orange, which may be cut into fractions. The advantage of using sheets of paper is that they show that the same unit may be divided into fractions of different values. The plan also enables the teacher to prove incidentally that the unit is equal to the sum of the fractions, and that

$$\tfrac{1}{2} = \tfrac{2}{4} = \tfrac{4}{8} \&c.$$

II. Examples.—Having shown what a fraction is, the next point is to show the notation by which it is represented. This is the purpose of the examples.

III. Parts.—It is important that a correct notion should be conveyed at the outset of the difference between the numerator and the denominator. The function of the denominator may be explained by showing that it is precisely the same as that of £ s. d., indicating different denominations of money. For example, 5d. is $\tfrac{5}{12}$ of a shilling; 9s. is $\tfrac{9}{20}$ of a pound.

IV. Kinds.—The nature of the improper fraction may also be shown in the concrete. Thus, 7s. 6d. is 15 sixpences, or $\tfrac{15}{2}$ of a shilling; but it is usual to represent it as $7\tfrac{1}{2}$ sh. An improper fraction, therefore, does not represent an impossible quantity, and is therefore not incorrect; but it is called "improper" because it represents more than a unit.

V. Application.—Under this head exercises are suggested on the lesson. These may be multiplied as occasion requires.

MODEL LESSON: SIMPLE SUBTRACTION.

INTRODUCTION.—Tell the children that, having learned how to add numbers together, they are now to learn how to take numbers away from each other.

HEADS.	MATTER.	METHOD.
DEFINITION.	The taking away of a smaller number from a larger to find what is left.	Illustrate on ball frame, or with marbles, nuts, pebbles, buttons, or any other convenient articles. Multiply such illustrations until the process is thoroughly understood. Always use examples of real objects, and vary them as much as possible.
EXAMPLES.	11 17 23 5 9 16 — — — 6 8 7	Let these and a number of similar examples be worked mentally; then put them down on the blackboard, and show the principle of adding and carrying; and thus prepare the children for its application in a larger sum.
RULE.	Write the larger number above the smaller, and *take* the latter *from* the former, figure by figure.	Avoid such words as subtrahend and minuend. Call the lines "larger" and "smaller," or "upper" and "under."

PROCESS.	*From* five hundred and thirty-six *take* three hundred and seventy-eight.
	
	          10 10
	From.... 5 3 6
	Take.... 3 7 8
	         — — —
	Remainder 1 5 8
	           1 1
		First step.—Put down the sum as in Addition—remind the children that they must be careful to place the figures in their proper places,—*units* under *units*, *tens* under *tens*, &c.
		Second step.—Take 8 from 6, you cannot. Add 10 to the top figure; then 8 from 16 and 8 remains.
		Third step.—Carry 1 to the next bottom figure; 7 and 1 are 8. Take 8 from 3, you cannot. Add 10 to the top figure; then 8 from 13 and 5 remains.
		Fourth step.—Carry 1 to the next bottom figure; 3 and 1 are 4. Take 4 from 5 and 1 remains.

PROOF.	Add the answer or remainder to the under line, and if the working be correct their sum will be the same as the upper line.	Show that in Addition the answer required is the *sum* of certain numbers, but that in Subtraction the answer required is the *difference* between certain numbers.

NOTES OF LESSONS ON ARITHMETIC. 51

MODEL LESSON: REDUCTION OF MONEY.

HEADS.	MATTER.	METHOD.
DEFINITION.	The change of a quantity from one denomination to another without altering its value.	Illustrate by changing a penny into halfpence, a sixpence into pence, &c.
EXAMPLES.	Reduce 4d. to farthings. Reduce 4s. to pence. Reduce 40 farthings to pence. Reduce 40 pence to shillings.	How many farthings are there in a penny? *Ans.* 4. Then how many in 4d., 6d., 8d., &c. How many pence in a shilling? *Ans.* 12. Then how many in 4s., 5s., 6s., &c. How many pence do 4 farthings make? *Ans.* 1. Then how many pence do 40 farthings make, 48, 60, &c. How many shillings do 12 pence make? *Ans.* 1. Then how many shillings do 24 pence make, 48, 60, &c.
RULE.	To change from a higher to a lower denomination, *multiply;* from a lower to a higher, *divide.*	Remind the children that the number of the lower denomination must always be the *greater*, and that of the higher, the *less*; also, that multiplication gives a *larger* answer, and division a *smaller.*

PROCESS.	Descending.
	Reduce £5 to farthings.
	    20
	  100 shillings.
	    12
	 1200 pence.
	    4
	 4800 farthings.
	
	Ascending.
	Reduce 1273 farthings to pounds.
	4) 1273 farthings.
	12) 318 pence and ¼d. over
	20) 26 sh. and 6d. over.
	    1 £ and 6s. over.
	Answer—£1, 6s. 6¼d.
		Ask for the money table. There are 20 shillings in 1 pound; therefore there are 5 times 20 shillings in 5 pounds; and so on.
		
		One penny equals four farthings; therefore the number of pence in a sum must always be one-fourth of the number of farthings; and so on.

PROOF.	Reverse the operation.	Give a number of examples of both kinds.

MODEL LESSON: THE VULGAR FRACTION.

HEADS.	MATTER.	METHOD.
DEFINITION.	A fraction is one or more of the equal parts into which a unit or whole is divided.	Take three sheets of paper of the same size. Fold one sheet into two equal parts, one into three equal parts, and one into four equal parts. Explain that in each instance the sheet represents the whole or unit, and the folds represent the fractions or equal parts of which it is composed. Explain that "fraction" means a piece broken off.
EXAMPLES.	$\frac{1}{2}$ $\frac{2}{2}$ $\frac{1}{3}$ $\frac{2}{3}$ $\frac{3}{3}$ $\frac{1}{4}$ $\frac{2}{4}$ $\frac{3}{4}$ $\frac{4}{4}$	Explain that the first sheet is divided into *halves*, the second into *thirds*, and the third into *fourths*. Show how to express one of these parts, two, three, &c.
PARTS.	**Numerator:** the upper figure. **Denominator:** the lower figure.	Explain "denominator" as naming the value of the fraction, and "numerator" as showing the number of parts taken. Refer to sheet folded in four. Denominator shows number of folds in whole sheet; numerator shows how many of these folds are taken: example, $\frac{3}{4}$. Show that if all the parts be taken, the fraction then equals the whole; thus, $\frac{2}{2}=1, \frac{3}{3}=1, \frac{4}{4}=1$.
KINDS.	**Proper Fraction:** numerator smaller than denominator. **Improper Fraction:** numerator larger than, or the same as, denominator. **Mixed Fraction:** whole number and proper fraction.	Examples:— $\frac{3}{4}$ $\frac{5}{6}$ $\frac{3}{8}$ Show how to change an improper fraction $\frac{7}{4}$ $\frac{13}{6}$ $\frac{29}{8}$ into a mixed fraction, and a mixed fraction into an improper fraction. $1\frac{3}{4}$ $2\frac{1}{6}$ $3\frac{5}{8}$ Point out that the three mixed fractions in the example are equal to the three improper fractions respectively.
APPLICATION	Exercises on slates and black-board.	1. Ask the scholars to divide lines, squares, &c., into a given number of equal parts, and to express these in figures. 2. Ask for twelve examples of each kind of fraction. 3. Give a number of exercises on improper and mixed fractions.

GRAMMAR.

CHAPTER VIII.

NOTES OF LESSONS ON GRAMMAR.

THERE is a difference of opinion as to the propriety and utility of teaching Grammar to young scholars. Some writers maintain that it is a study beyond the powers of children; others hold that it is dry and uninteresting, and therefore yields no nourishment; others, that even when understood it leads to no practical result. Grammar, it is said, is based on speech; not speech on grammar: and many persons who never have learned grammar both speak and write correctly, while many who have spent years over grammar books can do neither. These are objections rather to bad methods of teaching grammar than to the study itself. There is no reason why it should be more difficult for a child to recognize different kinds of words than to recognize different kinds of trees, or the various features of land and water, or the different values of the same figure according to its place in numeration. Grammar may, in fact, be made both simple and interesting, by the use of right methods, and by avoiding the mistakes indulgence in which has earned for the subject a bad name. Nice distinctions, over-refinements, and the use of technical and classical terms, should be avoided. The simplest definitions and forms of classification should be employed. Grammar should, from the first and throughout, be based on and conjoined with Analysis; and Analysis should, as soon as possible, be linked on to Composition. If these points be attended to, there is no reason why the study should not be easy and useful, both in sharpening the wits and in giving command over the language in use.

1. THE NOUN.

This lesson is adapted to the earliest stage in teaching Grammar. It covers much more ground, however, than can be gone over in a single lesson. The first three heads must occupy the class for many weeks before the fourth and fifth heads are taken up. It is not advisable that the attention of children should be confined to the Noun exclusively during the first year of the grammar course. The noun is known by its function as a part of speech; that is, in connection with other words in a sentence. The foundation of grammar is, that the Sentence is the unit of speech. (See remarks on "Definition" in sect. 2, "The Parts of Speech.") The earliest lessons on grammar should therefore start with the Sentence. But children cannot know what a sentence is if they know no other part of speech than the noun. Besides, the function of the noun will be most readily understood by being compared and contrasted with the functions of other parts of speech—say of the verb and the adjective. A Comparative table, therefore, including the verb as well as the adjective and the pronoun, is given in this chapter. It is adapted to the same stage as that on the noun, and is intended to be used along with it.

The following are the heads of the lesson on the Noun:—

  I. EXAMPLES.
  II. DEFINITION.
  III. EXERCISE.
  IV. KINDS.
  V. INFLECTIONS.

I. **Examples.**—These follow the sentences given in the Introduction, and are to be used in making sentences of the same kind, combining a noun with a verb. The objects, persons, &c., named should be as varied as possible, in order to show how comprehensive is the word "thing" used in the definition.

II. **Definition.**—This, in the case of young children, should be as short and as simple as possible. It should be expressed in their own language, and should be free from technical terms and intricate constructions. It may be necessary to remind the scholars frequently that it is the *name* of the thing, and not the thing itself, that is the noun; and also that name-words are nouns only when they are used in sentences.

III. **Exercise.**—The teacher must be guided by his own judgment in regard to the best time for using this head, and the best way of doing so. As the form suggested is that adopted in the Inspector's Examination, it should not be too long delayed, and should be used constantly from day to day.

IV. **Kinds.**—The classification of nouns according to kind is not of much importance. It rests on logical more than on grammatical differences. Excepting the rule—which is not absolute—that proper names have no plural, there is nothing in inflection or in syntax that depends on the distinction. It is therefore undesirable to trouble young children with it; but so long as custom retains it in text-books and examinations, it will be necessary to introduce it at some stage.

V. **Inflections.**—The particulars under this head should be introduced gradually, in connection with the daily lessons on the noun. Case should be delayed as long as possible; and, in connection with gender and number, exceptions should not be taught at this stage.

2. THE PARTS OF SPEECH.

This is a Fourth Standard lesson. Its object is not to define each of the Parts of Speech. That must be done in separate lessons. (See "The Noun," sect. 1.) The object of the lesson is to show, first, that there are parts of speech; and, secondly, the principle on which words are classified. It will also serve as an introduction to Analysis.

The lesson is arranged under the following heads :—

I. DEFINITION.

II. EXAMPLE.

III. Division into Members.
IV. Division into Words.
V. The Classes of Words.

I. Definition.—The Introduction leads up to this. The chief point to insist on is, that there can be no proper classification of words except as they are used in sentences, and that this is what is meant by Parts of Speech. Grammar regards words as the elements of which speech is made up. What letters are to a word, what figures are to a number, words are to a sentence. Words are but fractions; the Sentence is the unit of speech.

II. Example.—Hence it follows that we can reach the parts of speech only by analyzing the sentence. The first example in the Model Lesson is a sentence; the second is not. The second is given to show that all combinations of words are not sentences, but that only such combinations are sentences as are complete statements—as make sense. It is only by examining and analyzing the complete sentence that we can discover the parts of speech.

III. Division into Members.—The first analysis of the sentence shows it to consist of two parts,—a *naming* part, and a *telling* or asserting part. It is not advisable, at this stage, to use such terms as "subject" and "predicate." They are not only difficult in themselves, but they also increase the difficulty of understanding the things which they name. It may be well to show incidentally that these parts cannot be discovered in the second form of words given in the example. As many sentences as possible should be analyzed in this way.

IV. Division into Words.—The next step is to analyze each of the two members into words: then we reach the parts of speech.

V. The Classes of Words.—The four classes of words developed in the sentence analyzed are the most important, and may be called the primary classes. The attention of children should be confined to these words for some time. Not till they have thoroughly mastered these should they proceed to the other or secondary classes.

3. THE COMPLEX SENTENCE.

This lesson belongs to Standard V. or VI. It should be carefully noted that the subject of the lesson is not the analysis of a particular complex sentence, but the complex sentence as a division of Analysis. The question it seeks to answer is, What is a complex sentence?

The heads under which it is arranged are these:—

    I. EXAMPLES.
    II. DEFINITION.
    III. PARTS.
    IV. KINDS OF CLAUSES.

I. **Examples.**—The method adopted is to take a simple sentence, and to expand two of its members into clauses, thereby making it complex. This shows that the simple and the complex sentence express the same meaning; the sole difference is in form. To make this point as clear as possible, it may be explained that there are three forms in which a member of a sentence may be expressed,—a word, a phrase, and a clause: for example, a *learned* man; a man *of learning;* a man *who is learned.*

II. **Definition.**—This follows naturally from the example. A complex sentence is really a simple sentence with clauses introduced.

III. **Parts.**—This head gives the particulars for a broad general analysis of the sentence. The examples are taken from the sentence in the first head.

IV. **Kinds of Clauses.**—This head relates to subordinate clauses. The classification adopted is the functional one, which is at once the simplest and the only correct one. The classification according to the part of speech of the introductory word— relative, pronominal, interrogative, conjunctive—multiplies the number of the kinds of clauses, while it really gives no help to the scholar. The great advantage of the functional classification is that it treats analysis in the same way as parsing, and makes the one throw light on the other.

MODEL LESSON: THE NOUN.

INTRODUCTION.—Write on black-board such short sentences as, "The sky is blue," "The sun shines," "The dog barks." Get the children to recognize *sky, sun, dog* as Name-words.

HEADS.	MATTER.	METHOD.
EXAMPLES.	Names of objects, of persons, of places, of animals, of qualities.	Ask for names of objects in the school-room, in the house, in the town; names of boys and girls in the school, in the family; names of places in the neighbourhood. Require sentences to be made containing these words: "Tell me something about the *desk*, the *map*, about *John Smith*," &c. All name-words are called Nouns.
DEFINITION.	A Noun is the name of a thing.	Show that "thing" includes object, person, place, &c. Show that the *word* "book" is a noun,—not the *object* book. Show that a name-word is a noun only when it is a part of speech; that is, when it is used in a sentence.
EXERCISE.	Point out nouns in reading lesson.	In every case ask *why* the word selected is a noun. Ask whether other words in the lesson are name-words.
KINDS.	**Common.**—Class names: boy, dog, town. **Proper.**—Individual names: Charles, Towser, Leeds. **Abstract.**—Names of qualities: whiteness, beauty.	Show that the name "boy" is *common* to all boys; "John," "Charles," "Henry," are the *property* of individuals. Ask what makes *chalk* useful,—its *whiteness*. Show that "chalk" and "whiteness" cannot be separated except by the mind: abstract nouns are mental nouns.
INFLECTIONS.	For **Number**,—boy, boys; man, men; class, classes. For **Gender**,—lion, lioness; lad, lass .... For **Case**,—father, father's, fathers'.	Write down sentences showing the change in each instance, and its effect on other words. Each of the inflections must be treated in a special lesson.

NOTES OF LESSONS ON GRAMMAR. 59

COMPARISON OF PARTS OF SPEECH.

Arrangement of Lessons.	THE VERB.	THE ADJECTIVE.	THE PRONOUN.
INTRODUCTION	Write sentences, and ask for the words in them that *tell*, or make statements.	Write sentences, and ask for the words in them that show the *kind* of things.	Write a sentence in which nouns are repeated, and then *put* Pro-nouns *in their places*.
EXAMPLES.	Expressing *doing*: Tom *struck* the horse. Expressing *being*: The sea *was* calm	Colour: a *brown* coat; *green* leaves. Size: a *large* house. Number: *twenty* men.	He, she, it, they, them, who, which, that, &c.
DEFINITION.	A Verb tells about doing or being.	An Adjective describes a thing.	A Pronoun stands for a noun.
PRACTICE	Point out Verbs in reading lesson.	Point out Adjectives in reading lesson.	Point out Pronouns in reading lesson.
KINDS.	Transitive Verbs; as, The horse *kicked* the boy. Intransitive Verb; as, The horse *runs*. Neuter Verb; as, The horse *is* wild.	Adjectives of Quality; as, good, rich, sweet, kind, beautiful. Adjectives of Quantity; as, much, ten. Adjectives of Distinction; as, a, the, this.	Personal Pronouns; as, I, he, she, they. Relative Pronouns; as, who, which, that. Interrogative Pronouns; as, who? what?
INFLECTIONS. (To be treated separately.)	Number: He speaks; they speak. Person: I speak; he speaks. Tense: I speak, I spoke, I start, I started. Mood: I speak; speak out. Voice: They speak French; French is spoken there.	Comparison: rich, richer, richest; good, better, best; beautiful, more beautiful, most beautiful.	Number: I, we; he, they. Gender: he, she, it. Case: he, his, him.

MODEL LESSON: THE PARTS OF SPEECH.

INTRODUCTION.—Take a pile of books: show that each is for its own purpose,—one for reading, another for arithmetic, another for geography, another for history, and so on. Show that in like manner each word in a sentence has its own purpose or use,—some name things, some describe things, some tell about doing, &c.

HEADS.	MATTER.	METHOD.
DEFINITION.	The parts of speech are words classified according to the work they do in sentences.	Show that a word is not a part of speech until it is used in speech; that is, in a sentence. The words in a spelling-list or in a dictionary are not parts of speech. The same word may at one time be one part of speech, and at another time another: for example, "grave," "light."
EXAMPLE.	1. "Wise men speak little." 2. "On the top of the hill."	Show that 1. is a complete sentence, but that 2. is not. The latter does not tell us anything.
DIVISION INTO MEMBERS.	1. **The thing spoken about**: "wise men." 2. **What is said about it**: "speak little." 1. Naming part. 2. Telling part.	Divide other simple sentences in the same way. Do not at first use the words "subject" and "predicate." Show that the phrase, "On the top of the hill," cannot be divided in this way.
DIVISION INTO WORDS.	"Wise" shows the *kind* of men: **Adnoun.** "Men" *names* persons: **Noun.** "Speak" *tells* what wise men do: **Verb.** "Little" shows *how* wise men speak: **Adverb.**	Treat other simple sentences in the same way. Ask such questions as, What does "wise" do? What does "speak" do?
THE CLASSES OF WORDS.	1. **Nouns**: naming words. 2. **Adnouns** or **Adjectives**: describing words. 3. **Verbs**: telling words. 4. **Adverbs**: words showing *how*. 5. **Pronouns**: words standing for nouns. 6. **Prepositions**: relating words. 7. **Conjunctions**: binding words. 8. **Interjections**: shouting-out words.	Each of these classes will require separate treatment in detail. Point out that as the adnoun or adjective is joined to the noun, so the adverb is joined to the verb. Give examples of these words in use, but confine the attention to the *use* in each case. Formal definitions need not be given.

MODEL LESSON: THE COMPLEX SENTENCE.

INTRODUCTION.—Explain the difference between "simple" and "complex," applied to a machine. Refer to simple rule of three, and double rule of three: the latter is "complex."

HEADS.	MATTER.	METHOD.
EXAMPLES.	Simple sentence:— A generous man IS REGRETTED at his death. Complex sentence:— A man *who is generous* IS REGRETTED *when he dies*.	Show that these two sentences make the same statement and mean the same thing. The great difference between them is, that the first sentence contains only one verb, while the second contains three verbs; but two of them are subordinate.
DEFINITION.	A complex sentence contains one principal clause, and one or more subordinate clauses.	Point out that a "clause" is a member of a sentence that contains a verb and a nominative within itself. Whenever a word or a phrase in a simple sentence is expanded into a clause, the sentence becomes complex.
PARTS.	Principal clause; as, A man is regretted. Subordinate clauses; as, Who is generous; when he dies. Link words; as, Who, when.	Explain that the principal clause is the only one that makes sense by itself. Show that the only link-words in the simple sentence are prepositions. The link-words in complex sentences are relatives and conjunctions. Compare "*at his death*" with "*when he dies.*"
KINDS OF CLAUSES.	Subordinate clauses are— 1. **Noun clauses**; as, He said *that he would go.* 2. **Adjective clauses**; as, This is the house *that Jack built.* 3. **Adverbial clauses**; as, He started *when he heard the news.*	Show that the difference is one of function, the different clauses being equivalent to a noun, an adjective, and an adverb respectively. A "complex sentence" is thus a sentence in which the parts of speech are in the form of clauses.

HISTORY.

CHAPTER IX.

NOTES OF LESSONS ON HISTORY.

THERE is no subject in the school course in connection with which Notes of Lessons are more serviceable, or more necessary, than with History. This is true whether the subject of the lesson be a particular reign; or a particular event, such as a battle; or the life of a great man. In all cases a mass of details has to be dealt with, which cannot be properly mastered, either by the teacher or by his class, unless they be carefully and methodically arranged.

Abundant material for this purpose may be found in the larger histories, and in books of reference. The teacher can hardly expect to prepare a satisfactory lesson-scheme if he draws his information solely from the school manual. The mistake must also be avoided of supposing that the Notes of a Lesson on History should consist merely of a chronological table. A glance at the Model Lessons following will show that they consist of a greater variety of matter, arranged in a different way.

It is not enough, however, that the matter be arranged in convenient order. The successful teaching of History depends to a large extent on the method adopted. Events must be treated, not as isolated facts, but in their interdependence, like links in a chain. No opportunity must be missed of demonstrating the relation of cause and effect: thereby both will be more easily understood and more readily remembered. A point of great importance is, to seize on a leading feature or tendency in a period, or in a character, and to show how it was developed and in what ways it manifested itself.

1. A REIGN.

The following are the heads most suitable for the analysis of a Reign :—

    I. BIRTH AND PARENTAGE OF THE SOVEREIGN.
    II. TITLE; that on which his right to the throne depended.
    III. REIGN; its length.
    IV. FAMILY; his wife and children.
    V. DEATH; its cause and time.
    VI. CHARACTER.
    VII. CHIEF EVENTS.
    VIII. STATUTES.
    IX. INVENTIONS, ETC.
    X. WARS.
    XI. NAMES OF NOTE.

Every reign need not embrace the whole of these heads. Indeed, it may not be possible always to find material for every one of them. In one reign there may be no important statutes to record; in another, no great inventions; in another, no serious wars. The teacher will not omit to call attention to the fact that a reign has two aspects;—the one personal, relating to the sovereign; the other national, relating to his people. In the Model Lesson, heads I.-VI. form the personal division, and heads VII.-XI. the national one. It might be found useful in practice to make each division the subject of a special lesson.

The head of most importance is that entitled **Chief Events.** Under it, all the leading occurrences of the reign should be mentioned in chronological order, notwithstanding that they may be again referred to under the special head of Statutes or of Wars. This head may be treated briefly, or it may be elaborated to almost any extent. It should not in any case, however, be allowed to take the form of a dry chronological catalogue. The aim should be to present pictures of the great events, whether in the form of outline sketches or with the details elaborated fully.

2. A BATTLE.

The following are the heads most suitable in treating of a Battle :—

    I. OBJECT: Why was it fought?
    II. TIME: When was it fought?
    III. PARTIES: What nations were involved?
    IV. LEADERS: Who commanded on each side?
    V. LOCALITY: Where was it fought?
    VI. DETAILS.
    VII. RESULT: Who gained the victory?
    VIII. EFFECT: What followed the victory?

The head requiring special attention is that of **Details**. Under it, the plan of the battle must be shown, and the points on which success turned. The number and the minuteness of the details given must vary with the state of advancement of the class.

3. A BIOGRAPHY.

The heads under which a Biography may be most conveniently arranged are the following :—

    I. DESCRIPTION: For what was the man famous?
    II. BIRTH: Time and place.
    III. EDUCATION.
    IV. CHIEF EVENTS OF LIFE.
    V. CHARACTER.
    VI. DEATH.

Under the head of **Education**, it is proper to mention not only a man's formal schooling, but also the whole of the training which prepared him for his life's work. Here, as in the case of Reigns, the most important head is that which embraces the **Chief Events** of the man's life. It is advisable, whenever it can be done, to divide the life into periods, and to summarize the chief facts or events in each period.

MODEL LESSON: EDWARD I.

HEADS.	MATTER.	METHOD.
BIRTH AND PARENTAGE.	1237.—Son of Henry III.	Refer to his absence in Palestine when his father died.
TITLE.	Hereditary succession.	Explain.
REIGN.	1272 to 1307: 35 years.	Compare with other reigns.
FAMILY.	Wives.—(1) Eleanor of Castile—(2) Margaret of France. Children.—Fifteen by first wife, and three by second—his son Edward succeeded him.	Show the descendants of Edward intermarried, causing the Wars of the Roses.
DEATH.	From natural causes while marching against Scotland—aged 70.	Tell the story of Edward's dying command.
CHARACTER.	Courageous, ambitious, decisive, merciful, affectionate, sagacious.	Show fondness for arms by wars, and affection by grief at the death of father and wife Eleanor.
CHIEF EVENTS.	Wales conq.—first English "Prince of Wales" (1284).. The Jews banished (1290) ... Scotland overrun—the Stone of Destiny removed to Westminster (1296).........	Tell the story of Edward at Caernarvon. Explain this as the result of prejudice. Show ground of Edward's claim—refer to Henry II. and William the Lion.
STATUTES.	The **Great Charter** confirmed, with an addition that no tax be levied without the consent of the Parliament—**Charter of Forests** confirmed (1297, 1300)—**Statute of Mortmain** (1297).	Show how the people were often illegally taxed at the king's pleasure—this cost Charles I. his throne and his life.
INVENTIONS, &c.	Striking clocks introduced—halfpence and farthings coined—windmills and paper introduced from the East.	Show that the warlike spirit of the times was adverse to the progress of invention.
WARS.	With **Wales.**—Llewelyn slain—David executed at London. With **Scotland.**—Defeat of Baliol and of Wallace—Execution of Wallace at London.	Describe the brave efforts of the Welsh to retain their independence. Show how Scotland was united with England under James I.
NAMES OF NOTE.	**Earls of Surrey and Pembroke,** generals in the Scottish wars. **Earls of Hereford and Norfolk,** opposed arbitrary taxes ...	Refer to Scottish wars. Refer to confirmation of charters.

COMPARISON OF REIGNS.

Arrangement of Lesson.	ELIZABETH.	CHARLES I.	WILLIAM III. AND MARY II.
BIRTH AND PARENTAGE.	1533.—Daughter of Henry VIII. and Anne Boleyn.	1600.—Son of James I. and Anne of Denmark.	1650.—Son of Prince of Orange. 1662.—Daughter of James II.
TITLE.	Hereditary succession.	Hereditary succession.	Invited by Parliament.
REIGN.	1558 to 1603: 45 years.	1625 to 1649: 24 years.	1689 to 1694: William to 1702.
FAMILY.	Never married.	Wife.—Henrietta Maria (France). Children.—Charles, James, Mary.	No children.
DEATH.	From natural causes—aged 70.	Beheaded—aged 48.	William, from accident, aged 52.
CHARACTER.	Sagacious, despotic, jealous, vain.	Self-willed, passionate, insincere.	Reserved, courageous, sagacious.
CHIEF EVENTS.	Protestant religion established—Drake sailed round the world—Mary, Queen of Scots, ex.	This reign was one long struggle between the King and the Parliament—it ended in civil war.	Massacre of Glencoe—Grand Alliance—death of James II. in France—Darien Expedition.
STATUTES.	Act of Supremacy—Act of Uniformity—Poor Law Act.	Petition of Right—Grand Remonstrance.	Toleration Act—Bill of Rights—Act of Settlement.
INVENTIONS, &c.	Stocking-frame—newspaper—potatoes and tobacco introduced.	Hackney coaches used—coffee introduced.	Fire-engines—Savery's steam-engine.
WARS.	(1) Spain; (2) Irish Rebellion.	(1) Spain; (2) France; (3) Civil War.	(1) Jacobites in Ireland; (2) French.
NAMES OF NOTE.	Leicester—Essex—Sidney—Drake—Ralegh—Shakespeare.	Laud—Buckingham—Strafford—Coke—Pym—Cromwell.	Sancroft—Tillotson—Dryden.

EXERCISES—REIGNS.

Matter for Notes of Lessons to be arranged on the plan of the Model Lesson.

ALFRED.

849, son of Æthelwulf—hereditary succession—871 to 901, 30 years—wife, Alswitha; children, Edmund, Edward, Ethelward, and three daughters—natural causes; aged 52—wise, thoughtful, systematic, skilful in war, learned, charitable—ravages of the Danes; hiding of Alfred; defeat of the Danes; peace of Wedmore; encouragement of learning; division of the country into counties, &c.; organized a militia system—a code of laws—lanterns, mode of measuring time by candles—with the Danes—Æthelred; Alfred's son-in-law.

RICHARD I.

1157, son of Henry II.—hereditary succession—1189 to 1199, 10 years—wife, Berengaria of Navarre; no children—wounded at the siege of the Castle of Chaluz, died a few days afterwards; aged 42 years—brave, fearless, indomitable will, the greatest military leader of the day—took part in the third crusade; shipwrecked and taken prisoner by Leopold of Austria; ransomed for 100,000 merks; quarrelled with Philip of France—(1) with Saladin, (2) with Philip of France, (3) with his vassal the lord of Limoges—Baldwin, Longchamp, Robin Hood, Fitz-Osbert.

HENRY VII.

1455, son of Edmund Tudor (Earl of Richmond), and the great-great-grandson of John of Gaunt (fourth son of Edward III.)—hereditary succession and right of conquest—1485 to 1509, 24 years—wife, Elizabeth of York (daughter of Edward IV.); children, Arthur, Henry VIII., Margaret, Mary—natural causes; aged 54 years—avaricious, cruel—he united by his marriage the rival houses of York and Lancaster; suppressed several insurrections; invaded France; re-established the Court of Star Chamber; made peace with Scotland; England suffered from the plague; extortions of Empson and Dudley; Statute of Fines; Poynings' Law; Magnus Intercursus—the *Great Harry* built; North America discovered by Cabot—various insurrections; invasion of France—Sir Edward Poynings, Lambert Simnel, Perkin Warbeck, John Morton.

MODEL LESSON: BATTLE OF QUEBEC.

INTRODUCTION.—Show how at this time the whole of North America was divided between England and France, and that each country was striving to increase its territory at the expense of the other.

HEADS.	MATTER.	METHOD.
OBJECT.	To take Quebec from the French.	Show the value of its position.
TIME.	September 12, 1759.	Explain: reign of George II.
PARTIES.	England against France.	Explain the policy of the Marquis Duquesne, who wished to keep in French hands the traffic between Canada and the lower Mississippi.
LEADERS.	English.—General Wolfe, a celebrated soldier who had taken part in the war of the Austrian Succession, 1740-48, and distinguished himself at Minden, 1759 . . . . French.—Marquis de Montcalm.	Refer to Pitt's selection of Wolfe, over many older men, because of his proved ability.
LOCALITY.	Heights of Abraham, on western side of Quebec.	Describe the position of Quebec—show locality on map.
DETAILS.	Wolfe sent with 8,000 troops and 22 ships to take Quebec—bombarded and destroyed the lower city—the upper city and citadel were unharmed—failed in his attack on the French camp north of the city—conveyed his army to the south side of the city by night in flat-bottomed boats—scaled the Heights of Abraham—surprised the French, and gained a brilliant victory.	Make a sketch on blackboard to show the relative positions of the two armies as given in "Royal History of England," p. 393—give prominence to the effects of the surprise on the French army—confusion—want of guns, &c.
RESULT.	Total defeat of the French—Wolfe slain on the field—Montcalm mortally wounded—died next morning.	Tell the story of Wolfe's dying words.
EFFECT.	Surrender of Quebec, September 18—conquest of Canada followed shortly afterwards.	Refer to subsequent prosperity and rapid development of Canada.

COMPARISON OF BATTLES.

Arrangement of Lesson.	BANNOCKBURN.	NILE.	WATERLOO.
OBJECT.	An attempt to relieve Stirling Castle.	To check Napoleon's advance in the East.	To overthrow Napoleon, who had again seized the French throne.
TIME.	June 24, 1314.	August 1, 1798.	June 18, 1815.
PARTIES.	England against Scotland.	England against France.	England and Prussia ag't France.
LEADERS.	English.—Edward II. Scots.—Robert the Bruce.	English.—Admiral Nelson. French.—Admiral Brueys.	English, Wellington; Prussian, French, Napoleon. [Blücher.
LOCALITY.	Bannockburn, near Stirling.	B. of Aboukir, Rosetta m. of Nile.	Waterloo, near Brussels.
DETAILS.	Scottish army, 40,000 — English army, 100,000 — the English cavalry fell into hidden pits full of sharp stakes and was routed — Bruce then charged the English ranks, and 20,000 Scottish camp followers appearing, the English fled, thinking this a fresh army.	Coming up with the French fleet after Napoleon had landed his army, Nelson commenced the attack — the battle lasted all night — Nelson was severely wounded — the French flag-ship blew up with the admiral and his crew of 1000 men.	French army, 80,000 — Allied army, 69,000 — Napoleon tried to prevent the union of the British and Prussian armies — Wellington resisted all his attacks from ten in the morning till five in the evening, when the Prussians arrived and the battle was won.
RESULT.	The most terrible defeat ever sustained by an English army — 50,000 slain and prisoners.	A complete naval victory — 9 French men-of-war taken, and 2 burned.	Total defeat of the French. During three days' fighting nearly 70,000 were slain.
EFFECT.	The independence of Scotland was secured.	The French army was imprisoned in Egypt.	Napoleon abdicated — was sent to St. Helena, where he died (1821).

EXERCISES—BATTLES.
Matter for Notes of Lessons to be arranged on the plan of the Model Lesson.

BATTLE OF AGINCOURT.

To enforce Henry the Fifth's claim to the French crown—October 25, 1415—England against France—English, Henry V.; French, the Constable of France—Agincourt, a village in the north of France—English army 15,000; French army 100,000; the attack was commenced by the English archers, who were defended by a wall of wooden pikes; then they fought with swords, Henry being in the thickest of the battle; the firing of the barns of a neighbouring village completed the rout—the Constable of France and 11,000 knights were slain; the English lost 1,600 men—the conquest of France.

DEFEAT OF THE SPANISH ARMADA.

To deal a death-blow to the Protestantism of Europe—July 19 to 30, 1588—Spain against England—English : Lord Howard, Sir Francis Drake, Sir Martin Frobisher, Sir John Hawkins; Spanish: Duke of Medina Sidonia—the Strait of Dover—English fleet, 191 small vessels; Spanish fleet, 132 large ships, having on board, besides their crews, nearly 20,000 soldiers and 2,630 brass cannon : the Spanish fleet was scattered by fire-ships, attacked by the English, and destroyed by storms—only 53 shattered vessels returned to Spain—Protestantism established in England.

BATTLE OF PLASSEY.

To punish the Nabob of Bengal for his barbarous treatment of English prisoners—June 23, 1757—England against Bengal—English, Lord Clive; Indian, the Surajah Dowlah—Plassey, 96 miles north of Calcutta—English army 3,100, of which 800 were English; Indian army 60,000; Clive selected a strong position, protected by a wood and a steep bank; the battle was confined to a cannonade all day; towards evening the forces of Meer Jaffier, the vizier, abandoned the Nabob's camp; Clive then hurled his whole force upon the enemy, and won the battle—complete defeat of the Indians; less than 100 of the English army slain—this victory laid securely the foundation of the English empire in India.

MODEL LESSON: LIVINGSTONE.

HEADS.	MATTER.	METHOD.
DESCRIPTION	The greatest of modern travellers.	Describe the efforts made by travellers to explore unknown regions.
BIRTH.	At Blantyre, 1813.	Show on map.
EDUCATION.	Spent his youth working in a cotton-mill—earned enough money in summer to maintain himself at Glasgow College in winter—studied medicine and divinity.	Show his great perseverance in obtaining an education under such difficult circumstances.
CHIEF EVENTS OF LIFE.	Went to South Africa as a medical missionary in 1840.	Show how his desire to go to China was frustrated by war.
	Married Mary Moffat, daughter of Dr. Moffat, the missionary............	Refer to her first as a missionary's daughter, and afterwards as a missionary's wife.
	Spent 12 years in the interior of Africa—discovered Lake Ngami and the Zambesi...	Describe the interior—show places on map.
	Journeyed 2,000 miles in the interior—emerged at St. Paul de Loanda—discovered the Victoria Falls on the Zambesi—returned to England, after 16 years absence, 1856	Trace route on map. Describe the honours he received: gold medals from the Geographical Societies of London and Paris.
	Sent out by Government to explore the Zambesi, and to inquire into the slave trade. Returned 1864.........	Tell how Livingstone was affected when he saw the horrors of the slave trade.
	Started on his last journey in 1865—explored Lake Tanganyika—reported to be dead—expeditions sent out in search of him—found at Ujiji by H. M. Stanley, 1871...	Describe the anxiety of his friends. Give some details of Stanley's expedition—the meeting of the white men, and Stanley's reception in England.
CHARACTER.	Persevering and devoted; self-possessed and courageous; filled with desire to alleviate suffering, and with sympathy for the oppressed; never shed human blood in all his travels—a true philanthropist.	Give instances in his life in which these features of his character were shown.
DEATH.	At Ilala, Central Africa, 1873—his body brought to England, 1874—buried in Westminster Abbey—many statues have been erected to his memory.	Describe his death, the conveyance of his body to England, and his public funeral.

COMPARISON OF BIOGRAPHIES.

Arrangement of Lesson.	MILTON.	NELSON.	WATT.
DESCRIPTION.	A great poet.	England's greatest sailor.	A great inventor.
BIRTH.	At London, 1608.	At Burnham Thorpe, 1758.	At Greenock, 1736.
EDUCATION.	Educated at St. Paul's School, London — graduate of Cambridge University.	Went to sea at the age of twelve years.	Delicate childhood — educated at home — experimented a great deal.
CHIEF EVENTS OF LIFE.	Wrote "Comus," "L'Allegro," "Il Penseroso," "Lycidas" — took the side of the Parliament, and was Foreign Secretary to the Commonwealth in 1649 — lost his eyesight in 1654 — wrote "Paradise Lost" and "Paradise Regained."	Sailed in an Arctic expedition, 1773 — lost his right eye, 1794 — took part at St. Vincent, 1797 — lost his right arm, 1798 — won the battle of the Nile, 1798 — attacked Copenhagen, 1801 — viscount, 1805 — defeated the French and Spaniards at Trafalgar, 1805.	Apprenticed to a mathematical instrument maker in London — became mathematical instrument maker to Glasgow University — patented an improved steam-engine, 1769 — set up engine-works, near Birmingham, 1775.
CHARACTER.	A great scholar — a sublime poet — an earnest champion of civil and religious liberty — a strict Puritan.	Daring in judgment and in action — strong sense of duty — tender-hearted and unselfish.	Learned, thoughtful, laborious, upright, generous, and simple-minded — a great inventor.
DEATH.	1674. Buried at St. Giles', Cripplegate, London — monument in Westminster Abbey.	Killed at Trafalgar — buried in St. Paul's Cathedral — numerous monuments have been erected to his memory.	1819. Statues have been erected to his memory in many large towns.

EXERCISES—BIOGRAPHIES.

Matter for Notes of Lessons to be arranged on the plan of the Model Lesson.

SIR WALTER RALEGH.

A celebrated navigator and author—at Hayes, Devonshire, 1552—educated at Oriel College, Oxford—introduced to Queen Elizabeth; fitted out an expedition to colonize Virginia; brought the tobacco plant and the potato from America 1584; assisted in the defeat of the Spanish Armada 1588; sent to the Tower for taking part in the Main Plot, 1603; wrote a *History of the World;* allowed to lead an expedition to America; failed in his object; again imprisoned—enterprising, chivalrous, honourable, poetical taste, classical writer—beheaded 1618, aged 66 years.

WILLIAM SHAKESPEARE.

The world's greatest dramatic poet—at Stratford-on-Avon, 1564—left school in his fourteenth year; joined his father in his business of glover and wool-comber—married in his eighteenth year; became an actor and a play-wright; remained in London till 1612; wrote in twenty-five years thirty-six original plays—possessed of a profound knowledge of human nature; great poetical power and inventive skill—died at Stratford 1616, aged 52 years.

SIR WALTER SCOTT.

The greatest of romantic novelists—at Edinburgh, 1771—bred as a lawyer with his father—collected ballads during visits to the south of Scotland; published *Minstrelsy of the Scottish Border;* appointed Sheriff of Selkirkshire; wrote his first poetical romance (*The Lay of the Last Minstrel*) 1805; purchased Abbotsford 1811; his first novel (*Waverley*) published 1814; his printer and publisher failed, 1826; in debt £130,000; resolved to clear off his debt by writing; his health gave way; struck down by paralysis; travelled abroad; returned home—the most famous writer of his age; possessed vast stores of antiquarian and historical knowledge, humorous, honourable, wise, affectionate—died at Abbotsford 1832, aged 61.

GEOGRAPHY.

CHAPTER X.

NOTES OF LESSONS ON GENERAL GEOGRAPHY.

GEOGRAPHY is a subject on which Notes of Lessons are very often asked for in Government examinations. The particular subject prescribed is usually taken from the year's work; and as it has thus occupied much of the teacher's attention, he should have abundance of material for his Notes ready to his hand. The peculiarity of geography is that it includes a large number of details, and it therefore necessitates a large number of heads and of subdivisions. This makes note-making very helpful in teaching geography, and it also makes geography an excellent subject for giving practice in note-making. There is necessarily considerable variety in the schemes required for geographical subjects; but the four Model Lessons given in the present chapter include nearly every item of information that is likely to be required. Very slight modifications will make one or another of them applicable to other geographical features that may be presented. It may be observed, that in Government examinations the heads under which a special subject is to be arranged are now generally mentioned in the paper.

1. A COUNTRY—ENGLAND.

The heads in this case are the following :—

        I. DESCRIPTION.
       II. SITUATION.
      III. SIZE.

IV. Physical Features.
V. Products.
VI. Trade and Manufactures.
VII. Towns.
VIII. Population.
IX. Government.
X. Religion.

Most of these heads speak for themselves, and it is unnecessary, therefore, to add detailed explanations. Special attention may, however, be called to the following :—

IV. **Physical Features.**—This head describes the coast, the mountains, the rivers, and the lakes, as well as the nature of the climate and the character of the soil.

V. **Products.**—These are arranged under the three heads of Animals, Vegetables, and Minerals.

VII. **Towns.**—These are grouped according to their chief industry or other striking feature.

It may be necessary to point out that this Model Lesson contains a great deal more material than could possibly be used in a single lesson. It may be regarded rather as the outline of a series of lessons. Some of the single heads, indeed, contain lessons for several days. The outline may be adapted for different stages by judicious selection and omission.

2. A CITY—LONDON.

The lessons on Cities are arranged under the following heads :—

I. Description.
II. Situation.
III. Size.
IV. Population.
V. For what Noted.
VI. History.

I. **Description.**—It is not intended that the city should be either minutely described or barely characterized as "fine," or "grand," or "picturesque." First, there should be mentioned the class to which the city belongs—as sea-port, river-port, manufacturing town, inland town, fortified town. Then its position relatively to other cities should be noted. And, lastly, it should be stated whether it is a capital or not.

II. **Situation.**—Whether on the sea-coast or on a river; in what country, province, or county.

III. **Size.**—The length and breadth of its area, or its extent in square miles.

IV. **Population.**—As it is difficult for children to attach definite ideas to large numbers, it is advisable to use familiar comparisons. For example, it is very instructive to know that the population of London is nearly the same as that of Scotland.

V. **For what Noted.**—This is the most important head in the lesson. It includes numerous subdivisions, as, buildings, bridges, docks, manufactures, commerce, parks, and government.

VI. **History.**—Under this head are mentioned historical events of importance connected with the city. It includes notes relating to its progress and position;—as, for example, in the case of London, when it became the capital; and in the case of Metz, when it was transferred from Germany to France, and when it was returned by France to Germany.

3. A MOUNTAIN RANGE—THE ALPS.

The heads under which the Notes on a Mountain Range are classified are the following:—

        I. DESCRIPTION.
        II. SITUATION.
        III. DIRECTION.
        IV. DIMENSIONS.
        V. PHYSICAL FEATURES.
        VI. HISTORY.

The only head which requires to be specially adverted to is—
V. Physical Features.—This embraces all the chief points of the lesson:—the highest peaks; the height of the snow-line above the sea-level; the great passes; the character of the valleys; if there are glaciers, their number, area, and other particulars; the chief rivers that rise and the lakes that occur in the mountains; their animals, and their mineral and vegetable products.

4. A RIVER—THE NILE.

The Notes of this lesson fall naturally under the following heads :—

    I. DESCRIPTION.
   II. BASIN.
  III. SOURCE.
  IV. COURSE.
   V. LENGTH.
  VI. MOUTH.
 VII. TRIBUTARIES.
VIII. TOWNS.
  IX. USES.

The most important of these heads are :—

IV. Course.—This includes all the particulars that relate to the body of the river—its bed, slope, current, direction, and volume. Care should be taken to show how these particulars depend on one another; how the speed of its current, the nature and direction of its course, and its volume, all are affected by the inclination or slope of its bed.

IX. Uses.—The particulars given under this head are practically of great importance, and they are capable of being employed with great effect for truly educative purposes. In modern times, and especially in a commercial community, the extent to which a river is used for navigation and for industrial purposes is more important than anything else that may be said about it.

MODEL LESSON: ENGLAND.

HEADS.	MATTER.	METHOD.
DESCRIPTION	An island country.	Compare Continental,&c.
SITUATION.	Southern part of the island of Great Britain—west of Europe.	Show value of position, centre of land of globe.
SIZE.	Length, 365 m.—breadth, 290 m.	Show on map.
PHYSICAL FEATURES.	Coast.—3,000 m.—much indented—good harbours.... Mountains.—Chief: Pennine, Cambrian, Devonian..... Rivers.—Numerous and navigable: Thames, Severn, &c. Lakes.—Few—chiefly in north.. Climate.—Mild and healthy... Soil.—Fertile and well cultivated	Show value of broken coast. Get names of chief summits. Show value of cheap water-travelling, &c. Describe "lake district." Give causes of climate. Show result of climate.
PRODUCTS.	Animals.—Horse, cow, sheep, pig—fox, badger, stag.... Vegetables.—Grain, hops, &c... Minerals.—Coal, iron, lead, tin, slate, black lead, salt..	Show great value of domestic animals. Give localities. Show value of abundant minerals.
TRADE AND MANUFACTURES.	Imports. — Raw material, grain, colonial produce.... Exports.—Manufactured goods and minerals.......... Manufactures.—Cotton, woollen, iron, silk, glass, &c.... Fisheries.—Herring, pilchard, oyster, salmon........	Show use of raw material for manufactures. Show superiority of English manufactures. Chief manufacturing country in world. Give localities.
TOWNS.	Capital.—London, richest and largest city in the world.. Cotton Towns.—Manchester, Oldham, Bolton, Bury.... Woollen Towns.—Leeds, Bradford, Halifax, Huddersfield. Iron Towns. — Birmingham, Wolverhampton, Sheffield, Rotherham, Merthyr Tydvil Earthenware Towns.—Stoke, Burslem, Hanley...... Ports. — London, Liverpool, Bristol, Hull, Newcastle, Southampton.........	Compare with Paris and other large towns. Show situation, and state extent of trade. Describe "Black Country"—show value of coal and iron being found together. Show position of "Potteries." Show on map, and describe the trade of each.
POPULATION.	23 million.	Compare density with Scotland and Ireland.
GOVERNMENT.	Limited monarchy.	Explain: Sovereign, Lords, and Commons.
RELIGION.	Protestant.	All sects are tolerated.

NOTES OF LESSONS ON GENERAL GEOGRAPHY.

COMPARISON OF COUNTRIES.

Arrangement of Lesson.	IRELAND.	FRANCE.	CANADA.
DESCRIPTION.	An island country.	A Continental country.	A British colony.
SITUATION.	West of Great Britain.	West of Europe.	Northern part of North America.
SIZE.	Length, 300 m.—breadth, 180 m.	Length, 660 m.—breadth, 615 m.	Length, 3000 m.—breadth, 2000 m.
PHYSICAL FEATURES.	Coast indented—mountains round coast—rivers slow and navigable—lakes numerous—climate moist—soil fertile and boggy.	Coast not much indented—mountains few; very high on frontiers—rivers large—lakes few—climate delightful—soil fertile.	Coast extensive, partly ice-bound—mountains in west—rivers numerous—lakes, largest known—climate varied—soil fertile.
PRODUCTS.	Few animals—wheat, oats, potatoes, flax—coal, copper, iron.	Bear, wolf, boar, eagle—large forests, extensive vineyards—iron and coal.	Bison, bear, wolf, beaver — immense forests—gold, iron, lead, tin, petroleum.
TRADE AND MANUFACTURES.	Imports: manufactured goods—exports: farm and dairy produce—manuf.: linen, cotton.	Imports: raw goods and colonial produce — exports: manufactured goods — manufactures: silk, iron, jewellery.	Imports: manufactured goods—exports: forest and farm produce—fisheries very important; chiefly cod.
TOWNS.	Dublin, Belfast, Cork, Limerick, Waterford, Londonderry.	Paris, Lyons, Marseilles, Bordeaux, Lille, Nantes.	Ottawa, Quebec, Montreal, Toronto, Halifax, Fredericton.
POPULATION.	About 5½ million.	About 36 million.	About 4 million.
GOVERNMENT.	Constitutional, under Queen of England.	Republican.	Constitutional, under Governor-General representing the Queen.
RELIGION.	Chiefly Roman Catholic.	Roman Catholic.	Protestant and Roman Catholic.

EXERCISES—COUNTRIES.

Matter for Notes of Lessons to be arranged on the plan of the Model Lesson.

SCOTLAND.

An insular country—northern part of Great Britain—length 288 miles; breadth from 18 to 150 miles—coast 2500 miles; mountainous, chief range the Grampians; rivers short and rapid, Clyde, Forth, Tweed, Tay; lakes numerous and beautiful, Lomond, Katrine; colder climate than that of England; soil well cultivated—stag, fox, &c.; horse, cow, sheep, pig; wheat, oats, barley, rye, potatoes; coal, iron, lead, stone, slate—raw material, food, colonial produce; manufactured goods; cotton, linen, woollen goods, machinery; salmon, herring, &c. —Edinburgh, Glasgow, Dundee, Aberdeen, Greenock, Paisley—3½ million—limited monarchy—Protestant.

PALESTINE.

A continental country, also called the Land of Canaan, the Land of Promise, the Holy Land, the Land of Israel, and the Land of Judah—south-west of Asia, bordering the Mediterranean—length 200 miles, breadth 70 miles—coast low and regular; mountains in north, chief Lebanon; rivers, only one of importance, the Jordan; lakes, Waters of Merom, the Sea of Galilee, the Dead Sea; climate mild; soil productive—panther, hyena, jackal, bear, fox; camel, horse, &c.; wheat, barley; figs, olives, &c.; iron, copper, asphalt—manufactured goods, especinlly cotton; the produce of the soil; no manufactures of importance—Jerusalem, Bethlehem, Hebron, Nazareth—Jews, Turks, Greeks, Arabs, &c.—under Turkish rule—Mohammedan.

INDIA.

A continental country—a peninsula in the south of Asia—length 1900 miles, breadth 1800 miles—coast not much indented; mountainous in north, chief range the Himalaya; chief rivers, Ganges, Brahmapootra, Indus; lakes, not important; climate varied, affected by periodical winds; soil fertile—elephant, tiger, rhinoceros, crocodile, &c.; palm, banyan, cotton; rice, tea, coffee, &c.; precious stones, gold, silver, copper, tin, iron, coal—manufactured goods; raw material; shawls, silk, cotton goods—Calcutta, Bombay, Madras, Benares, Delhi, Lucknow—184 million—under a viceroy representing the Queen, who is Empress of India—chiefly Mohammedan.

NOTES OF LESSONS ON GENERAL GEOGRAPHY.

MODEL LESSON: LONDON.

INTRODUCTION.—Point out on maps of England, Europe, and World.

HEADS.	MATTER.	METHOD.
DESCRIPTION	A sea-port town—the largest and richest city in the world—the capital of the British Empire.	Compare with Paris, Vienna, Pekin.
SITUATION.	On both banks of the Thames, 60 miles from the sea; in parts of Middlesex, Surrey, and Kent.	Show value of position: navigable river, &c.—centre of land surface of world.
SIZE.	12 miles long and 10 miles broad—30,000 miles of streets.	Compare with some place in locality.
POPULATION	Above 3 million.	Compare with population of Scotland.
FOR WHAT NOTED.	**Buildings.**—St. Paul's Cathedral, Westminster Abbey, the Tower, Houses of Parliament, &c............	Give historical associations and present uses of buildings.
	Bridges.—15; principal, London Bridge, cost £2,000,000.	Describe daily traffic on London Bridge.
	Docks.—Have 4 miles of river frontage.	Show importance: 20,000 vessels enter and depart yearly.
	Manufactures.—Silk-weaving, ship-building, sugar-refining, watch-making, tanning, coach-making, iron and steel works, immense breweries. .	Show that varied manufactures must grow out of the wants of such a crowded city.
	Commerce.—Not only greater than that of any other city, but greater than that of many countries.	Explain that many wholesale merchants have their head-quarters in the city.
	Parks.—Numerous.	Called "the lungs of London." Show why.
	Government.—Lord mayor, 25 aldermen, 206 councillors.	Explain the functions of the several officials.
HISTORY.	Called Llyn-Din by the Saxons.	"The town on the lake."
	Colonized and fortified by the Romans.............	Tell about Roman occupation of Britain.
	Destroyed by Boadicea, 61.	Describe her wrongs.
	Rebuilt and walled by the Romans, 306..........	Show growing importance of the city.
	Pillaged by the Danes, 839.	Tell who Danes were.
	Made the capital of England during the Norman period.	Refer to coronation of Norman kings
	First charter granted by William I., 1079..........	Explain "charter."
	The Great Plague, 1665.	Describe its terrible effects: give causes.
	The Great Fire, 1666.	Describe its extent.

COMPARISON OF CITIES.

Arrangement of Lesson.	GLASGOW.	DELHI.	METZ.
DESCRIPTION.	A sea-port town—the largest city in Scotland.	An inland town—a celebrated city of British India.	A fortified town—the chief town of Lorraine.
SITUATION.	On the river Clyde.	On tributary of the river Jumna.	On the Moselle.
SIZE.	About 3 miles from east to west—area, 9 square miles.	Circumference, 7 miles.	
POPULATION.	547,000.	154,000.	51,000.
FOR WHAT NOTED.	Ancient cathedral, university, Royal Infirmary, Royal Exchange, four public parks, large shipping—chief port and manufacturing town in Scotland—famous for iron ship-building—largest chemical works in the world—centre of coal district.	Red granite wall entered by 11 gates, Mogul's palace, mosque, Hindu temples, college—ruined tombs, gardens, and palaces show site of ancient city—Cashmere shawls are embroidered in silk and gold—goldsmiths' work famous for its beauty.	Citadel, armoury, hospital, barracks, arsenals, powder mill, military schools—Gothic cathedral, with beautiful spire 373 feet high—university—public library—manufactures, woollen cloths, muslins, lace, glass.
HISTORY.	King William the Lion made it into a burgh in 1190—only fifteen hundred inhabitants, 1300—first stone bridge built, 1345—university established, 1451—first steamboat sailed on the Clyde, 1812.	Once the capital of India—a million inhabitants, 1700—taken by the British, 1803—seized by sepoy mutineers, 1857—besieged and taken by the British, 1857—Queen Victoria proclaimed Empress of India, 1877.	A free city in the tenth century—taken by the French, 1552—besieged by Charles V., 1552-3—ceded to France, 1648—besieged by the Germans in August 1870—capitulated in October 1870—returned to Germany by the treaty of Frankfurt.

EXERCISES—CITIES.

Matter for Notes of Lessons to be arranged on the plan of the Model Lesson.

EDINBURGH.

The capital of Scotland—built on ridges of hills; about a mile from the Firth of Forth—population about 212,000—Old and New Town, Castle, Holyrood Palace, two Cathedrals, University, Fine-Art Galleries, New Infirmary, various hospitals, monuments, &c.; printing and publishing centre, railway centre; beautiful public gardens and parks; Lord Provost, Bailies, Councillors—made metropolis of Scotland by James III. 1482; Holyrood Palace built by James IV.; Mary Queen of Scots made Holyrood her residence 1561; James VI. left Edinburgh as king of England 1603.

DUBLIN.

A sea-port town; the capital of Ireland—on the Liffey, at its entrance into Dublin Bay—about 9 miles in circumference—population about 300,000—Castle, Courts of Law, College, Custom House, Bank of Ireland, two Cathedrals, various hospitals, numerous monuments, &c.; nine bridges; large docks; exports linens, poplins, provisions, porter; 613 vessels engaged in the sea-fishery; Lord Mayor and 45 Councillors—Christianity introduced by St. Patrick about 448; walls built 798; taken by English 1170; assembly of Irish princes, who swore allegiance to King John 1210; James II. proclaimed king 1689; rebellion 1798; Industrial Exhibition 1853; Fine-Art Exhibition 1861.

JERUSALEM.

The capital of Palestine—built on hills; 18 miles from the river Jordan—population about 20,000—walls of hewn stone, crowned by battlements, entered by gates; narrow, ill-paved streets; city divided into four quarters, Moslem, Christian, Armenian, Jewish; Mosque of Omar on site of Solomon's Temple; Church of the Holy Sepulchre; various convents, synagogues, &c.; extensive bazaars, little commerce; governed by the Turks—partly taken by Joshua from the Jebusites; destroyed by Nebuchadnezzar; rebuilt by command of Cyrus; held as a Roman city under Herod, who restored the Temple; destroyed by the Romans under Titus; under Turkish government for about 700 years.

NOTES OF LESSONS ON GENERAL GEOGRAPHY.

MODEL LESSON: THE ALPS.

HEADS.	MATTER.	METHOD.
DESCRIPTION	The chief mountains in Europe.	Compare with others.
SITUATION.	Central and Southern Europe, occupying parts of France, Switzerland, Italy, Austria, and Turkey..........	Let the children point out the different sections of the Alps on the map.
DIRECTION.	North and north-east, from Mediterranean to Danube..	Compare with courses of rivers.
DIMENSIONS.	Length, nearly 600 miles— breadth, about 100 miles...	Compare with size of Great Britain.
PHYSICAL FEATURES.	**Peaks.**—Mont Blanc, 15,744 feet (*highest in Europe*)—Monte Rosa, 15,174 feet...	Compare with Snowdon, Ben Nevis, &c.
	Snow-line.—Between 9,000 and 10,000 feet.............	Explain "snow-line."
	Passes.—Great St. Bernard, 8,150 feet—Mont Cenis—Simplon—Mont St. Gothard—Splügen.............	Explain "pass;" tell about St. Bernard dogs.
	Valleys.—Varied, some long and wide, others narrow and rocky, containing lakes....	Describe the villages, &c., of the Alpine valleys.
	Glaciers.—About 400—cover 1,400 square miles—descend to 3,400 feet above the sea. .	Explain "glacier;" name rivers which have their sources in glaciers.
	Rivers.—Danube, Rhine, Rhone, Inn, Drave, Save, Po.	Point out sources and directions on map.
	Lakes.—Very beautiful—Constance, Geneva, Lucerne...	Point out and describe.
	Animals.—Eagle, hawk, chamois, marmot, wolf, bear....	Describe chamois-hunting.
	Minerals.—Iron, copper, lead, coal, quicksilver, rock-salt, precious stones, and some gold and silver..........	
	Vegetation.—Vine, maize, and chestnut to 2,000 feet—grain, beech, and oak to 4,000 feet.	Show how vegetation becomes scantier the higher we go. Compare with Arctic regions.
HISTORY.	Mont Blanc first ascended 1787.	Describe an ascent.
	Napoleon crossed by the Great St. Bernard pass in 1800...	Tell about this.
	Roads over Mont Cenis and the Simplon made by Napoleon, 1801–6..............	Describe these.
	Mont Cenis Tunnel made 1857–1871................	Describe the work and its value.
	Railway over Mont Cenis, constructed 1867..........	Describe process.

COMPARISON OF MOUNTAIN RANGES.

Arrangement of Lesson.	GRAMPIANS.	ANDES.	HIMALAYA.
DESCRIPTION.	Chief mountains in Scotland.	Chief mountains in S. America.	Chief mountains in Asia.
SITUATION.	The centre of Scotland.	On the western coast of S. America.	Between India and Tibet.
DIRECTION.	North-east to south-west, from Aberdeenshire to Argyleshire.	North to south, from the Isthmus of Panama to Cape Horn.	South-east to north-west, from the Brahmapootra river to the Hindoo Koosh mountains.
DIMENSIONS.	Length about 80 miles—breadth from 10 to 30 miles.	Length, 4,500 miles — breadth, from 40 to 400 miles.	Length, about 1,500 miles—breadth, from 100 to 160 miles.
PHYSICAL FEATURES.	Ben Nevis, the highest peak, 4,406 feet high—150 feet below snow-line—wild and rugged—glens, picturesque—rivers, Findhorn, Spey, Don, Dee, Forth, Tay, Esk—lakes noted for size and beauty, chief Loch Lomond—minerals, chiefly stones—animals, deer—vegetation, good.	Aconcagua, the highest peak, 23,200 feet. Volcanic—snow-line, near the equator, 15,800 feet—glaciers in south—passes very elevated — valleys high, long, and enclosed—high table-land—chief river, the Amazon —lakes, few—minerals, various —vegetation, varied.	Mount Everest, the highest mountain in the world, 29,002 feet—snow-line, about 16,000 feet—passes, very elevated — deep gorges — glaciers found on every part—chief rivers, the Ganges, Indus, and Brahmapootra—lakes, few—minerals, few—animals, abundant — vegetation, varied.
HISTORY.	It is said that at Ardoch the Caledonians under Galgacus were defeated by the Romans under Agricola.	Chimborazo, a cone-shaped summit, 21,063 feet high, was long regarded as the highest mountain in the world — it was ascended in 1856.	The highest point has never been reached — the great glacier of the range, called Ibi-Gamin, 22,000 feet high, was ascended in 1855.

EXERCISES—MOUNTAIN RANGES.

Matter for Notes of Lessons to be arranged on the plan of the Model Lesson.

PYRENEES.

An extensive mountain range of Europe—between France and Spain—direction, south-south-east to north-north-west—length 270 miles, breadth from 50 to 100 miles—principal summit, Maladetta, 11,168 feet; snow-line, between 8000 feet and 9000 feet; numerous passes; no true glaciers have been discovered; chief rivers, Adour, Garonne, and Aude; iron, copper, lead, rock-salt; bear, lynx, &c.; maize to 3280 feet, pine to 10,870 feet—the Peace of the Pyrenees concluded between France and Spain 1659; Soult defeated by Wellington, 1813, crossed the Pyrenees, and retreated into France; railway through the Pyrenees opened 1862.

APENNINES.

A mountain range of Southern Europe—runs throughout the whole length of Italy—direction north-west to south-east—length about 800 miles—principal summit, Monte Corno, 9543 feet high; thirteen passes; valleys open into extensive plains; volcanic, Vesuvius (4165) the only active volcano in Europe; rivers, Arno, Tiber; small quantities of iron, celebrated marble quarries; the most part of the range is barren; near Genoa and Naples, figs, oranges, &c.

BALKANS.

A mountain system of European Turkey—between Roumelia and Bulgaria—direction south and east—length about 200 miles—average height 4000 feet, highest peak Tchar-Dagh, 9700 feet; several passes, the principal, the Gate of Trajan; deep and narrow gorges; vegetation more luxuriant in east—Shipka pass, forced by Russians 1877.

URAL MOUNTAINS.

A mountain system of the Russian Empire—between Europe and Asia—direction north to south—length about 1300 miles, breadth from 16 to 66 miles—several peaks 5000 feet high; slope often gentle, one good carriage-road; chief river the Petchora; rich in minerals, gold diggings occur on both slopes; platinum is obtained from Nijui-Tagilsk; rich copper ores; nearly five million tons of iron were extracted in 1862; various precious stones.

NOTES OF LESSONS ON GENERAL GEOGRAPHY. 87

MODEL LESSON: THE NILE.
INTRODUCTION.—Refer to the finding of Moses.

HEADS.	MATTER.	METHOD.
DESCRIPTION	The most remarkable river in the world; the largest in Africa.	Give brief history, ancient and modern.
BASIN.	Boundaries. — The Sahara, Abyssinia, Red Sea. District.—North-eastern Africa, comprising the whole of Egypt and Nubia.	Make a sketch on blackboard. Explain that in the Bible the Nile is called "the river of Egypt."
SOURCE.	Victoria Nyanza and Albert Nyanza, two great lakes lying across the Equator—3,740 feet above the sea-level.	Tell about their discovery by Captains Grant, Speke, and Burton, and Sir Samuel Baker.
COURSE.	Bed.—Of rich mud. Slope.—Steep, seven cataracts Current.—Varied velocity. Direction.—Northerly—winding in the earlier part. Volume.—Varied; greatly increased during inundation.	Explain how the *slope* of a river's bed affects the speed of its current and the direction of its course. Give examples of rapid rivers and slow rivers, showing causes.
LENGTH.	Total.—4,000 miles (including all its windings). Direct course, 2,350 miles. Navigable.—By steamers about 90 miles.	Compare with Mississippi. Show the interruptions caused by cataracts.
MOUTH.	Sea.—Mediterranean. Mouths.—Four: extreme ones, Rosetta and Damietta. Delta.—Form of a triangle.	Only African river that reaches this sea. Explain "Delta;" same shape as Greek letter Δ, which is so called.
TRIBUTARIES	R. Bank.—Blue Nile, Atbara. L. Bank.—No importance.	Show character of country.
TOWNS.	Alexandria. — Chief commercial port of Egypt. Damietta.—Noted for rice fields. Cairo. — Capital of Egypt — largest town in Africa — near great pyramids. Khartoum.—Capital of Nubia —centre of caravan traffic.	Mention ancient remains; Nelson's victory, 1798. Show value of rice. Describe pyramids. Show how trade is carried on by caravans.
USES.	Annual inundation. — Renders Egypt habitable — causes valley of Nile to be very fertile. Navigation.—Chief means of communication. Fisheries.—Abundant.	Explain this — refer to sowing bread on waters, and finding it after many days (Eccl. xi. 1). Explain that there are no roads and no railways. Used for food.

COMPARISON OF RIVERS.

Arrangement of Lesson.	THAMES.	VOLGA.	AMAZON.
DESCRIPTION.	The longest river in England.	The longest river in Europe.	The largest river in the world.
BASIN.	Boundaries. — Chiltern Hills, Cotswold Hills, Salisbury Plain, North Downs. District. — Seven counties.	Boundaries. — Valdai Hills, Ural Mountains, Steppes of Russia. District. — The whole of central and eastern Russia.	Boundaries. — The Andes, mountains of Brazil, Parimé mts. District. — The north-eastern portion of South America.
SOURCE.	Cotswold Hills, in Gloucestershire — 376 feet above the sea.	A small lake in the Valdai Hills, 550 feet above the sea.	A lake in the Andes, about 14,000 feet above the sea.
COURSE.	Gravel and chalk — gradual — slow — easterly — large and uniform.	Sandy — gradual — slow — southerly, then easterly — very great.	Muddy — steep — rapid — easterly — immense.
LENGTH.	250 miles — tidal, 80 miles — navigable, 70 miles.	2,400 miles — not subject to tides — navigable, its whole course.	4,000 miles — tidal, 500 miles — navigable, about 3,000 miles.
MOUTH.	Enters the North Sea — width of mouth, 15 miles.	Enters the Caspian Sea by upwards of 60 mouths.	Enters the Atlantic by two mouths.
TRIBUTARIES.	R. B. — Kennet, Wey, Medway. L. B. — Windrush, Colne, Lea.	R. B.: Oka, Sura. — L. B.: Tvertza, Mologa, Sksksna, Kama.	Right Bank. — Madeira. Left Bank. — Rio Negro.
TOWNS.	London, Richmond, Windsor, Reading, Oxford.	Astrakhan, Saratov, Nijni-Novgorod, Moscow (on tributary).	Barra, La Paz, Santa Cruz, Cochabamba (all on tributaries).
USES.	Of great commercial importance. More than 20,000 vessels enter or leave the port in a year.	The great highway of Russian commerce — valuable fisheries.	The inland navigation of the Amazon and its tributaries is about 50,000 miles.

EXERCISES—RIVERS.

Matter for Notes of Lessons to be arranged on the plan of the Model Lesson.

GANGES.

A celebrated river of India—Himalaya Mountains, Vindhya Mountains; north-east of India, comprising North-West Provinces, Nepaul, Oudh, parts of Bengal, and several other provinces—in glaciers in the Himalaya, nearly 14,000 feet above the sea—varied course; south-easterly direction—length 1514 miles; tidal 160 miles; navigable about 150 miles—meets Brahmapootra and enters Bay of Bengal by many mouths, fourteen of which are navigable, principal, the Ganges and the Hooghly; delta considerable; a low marshy district near the mouth called the Sunderbunds—Jumna, Sone; Gumti, Ghogra—Calcutta, Delhi, Agra, Allahabad, Benares, Lucknow—inland navigation; regarded as sacred by the Hindus.

SEVERN.

One of the principal rivers of England—Cambrian mountains, Wrekin, Cotswold hills; Montgomeryshire, Shropshire, Worcestershire, Gloucestershire—in a small lake on the east side of Plinlimmon, 1500 feet above the sea—steep and rapid; north-east, south-east, and south—length 180 miles; navigation bad, a canal has been cut from Gloucester to the sea; joined to most of the rivers of central England by canals—flows into Bristol Channel; the tidal wave, called the "bore," rushes into the Severn with such violence that the stream rises suddenly to a great height—Terne, Wye, Usk, Taff; Terne, Stour, Upper and Lower Avon—Montgomery, Shrewsbury, Worcester, Tewkesbury, Gloucester, Hereford, Monmouth, Rugby, Warwick, Bath, Bristol—provides internal communication.

ST. LAWRENCE.

The chief river in Canada—forms part of the northern boundary of the United States—western tributaries of Lake Superior—passes through the great lakes of North America; Lake Superior, the largest fresh-water lake in the world; between Lakes Erie and Ontario are the great Falls of Niagara—length 2150 miles; tidal 350 miles; navigable for large vessels 500 miles—enters the Bay of St. Lawrence by a mouth 100 miles wide—chief tributary the Ottawa —Detroit, Buffalo, Montreal, Quebec—the river and its lakes form a great highway of commerce extending 2000 miles inland.

GEOGRAPHY.

CHAPTER XI.

NOTES OF LESSONS ON PHYSICAL GEOGRAPHY.

ACCORDING to the usual method of instruction, and to the requirements of the Education Code, the earliest lessons in Geography are lessons on Physical Geography. Young children are taught about the form and motions of the Earth, the meaning of a map, and general definitions, before they are taught the geography of their own country, or of any part of the world. This may be objected to as an inversion of the natural process—as putting the abstract before the concrete, the general before the particular; but since the prescribed course must be followed, it is the more necessary that its difficulties should be as far as possible removed. There is, therefore, here a very obvious case for the careful preparation and the systematic use of Notes of Lessons. There is a further need for this in the fact that such subjects cannot be taught to elementary classes from text-books alone. They must be taught by simple oral explanations, and with the help of models and diagrams. The success of the oral teaching will depend on the care with which the material is gathered and arranged in notes. In a subject so varied as physical geography, and embracing so many different features, it is impossible to obtain uniformity of plan in the division and arrangement of the notes. Each of the Model Lessons in this chapter involves a different arrangement of heads. Four lessons are given, on the following subjects:—the Form of the Earth, a Map, Climate, and Tides. The first two belong to an early stage, and may be given to Standard II. The last two are sufficiently advanced for those standards which take up specific subjects.

1. THE FORM OF THE EARTH.

The heads in this case are only two :—

    I. Definition.
    II. Proofs.

The latter, however, contains numerous subdivisions, which form a sufficiently extended lesson. The proofs of the Earth's roundness given in the lesson are six in number. They begin with the simplest, and are arranged in the order of difficulty. The teacher should select only such proofs as he deems suited to the intelligence of his class.

2. A MAP.

The heads under which this lesson is arranged are the following :—

    I. Definition.
    II. Directions.
    III. Lines.
    IV. General Features.
    V. Uses.

I. **Definition.**—In this case this head contains the gist of the lesson. The teacher's chief object should be to make the children understand "the meaning of a map." The "definition" is expressed in simple enough language, but it should not be presented to the class until the "method" has been exhausted. The whole value of this part of the lesson lies in the method, which should lead up to the definition, as the definition sums up the teachings of the method.

II. **Directions.**—Namely, North, South, East, and West. The "method" here will show the convenience of being able to describe in this way the direction of one place from another.

III. **Lines.**—This head relates specially to the lines of Latitude and Longitude. In explaining their use, it must be made clear that both are necessary in order to define the position of a place, as a point is the intersection of two lines. There are other lines on maps, such as the Tropics, the Arctic and Antarctic Circles; but their use belongs to the globe as a whole, rather than to sectional maps. Differences of latitude and longitude are measured in degrees, of which there are 360 in every circle, whether large or small. In this connection the children may be made to understand the meaning of "scale"— how a small map and a large one may represent the same portion of the Earth's surface. Let the teacher draw two circles on the black-board, the one very much larger than the other, and divide each of them into four parts; and then show that the picture of England must be much larger in the one case than in the other. On some maps lines are drawn at right angles to one another, and indicate measurements in English miles.

IV. **General Features.**—This head has reference to the marks used to represent the coast line of a country, and its mountains, rivers, and towns. Allusion may also be made to the coloured lines used to separate one country from another, and also to distinguish provinces or counties.

V. **Uses.**—This head may be made to aid the main purpose of the lesson, if care be taken to show that, in noting the various uses of a map, we may obtain a very clear idea of what a map is and means.

3. CLIMATE.

This lesson is arranged under the following heads :—

I. DEFINITION.
II. CAUSES OF CHANGE.

I. **Definition.**—This head aims at showing what Climate is; that is, what we mean when we speak of the climate of a place. Reference is made to two points in the definition ;—first, *temperature*, or degree of heat or cold ; secondly, *moisture*, or degree of wetness or dryness.

II. **Causes of Change.**—The object of this head is to enumerate and explain the causes which account for the difference in climate of different places. It should be noted that the climate of a particular place or region is the result, not of one cause, but of several causes. For example, latitude and elevation produce the same effects; but for that very reason they tend to destroy each other's influence. The effect of a low latitude is counteracted by the effect of a high altitude. Chimborazo is near the equator, but its top is covered with perpetual snow. Thus, also, all the gradations of climate between the equator and the poles may be exhibited on a mountain side. The base of Chimborazo has a tropical climate, that of its summit is arctic, while temperate regions lie between.

4. TIDES.

The Notes of this lesson are arranged under three heads :—

    I. DEFINITION.
    II. CAUSES.
    III. THE TIDE-WAVE.

I. **Definition.**—The fact stated in the definition or description of the Tides will be well known to all children who have lived at the sea-side. Others must accept the fact on their testimony. The important point in the lesson is the next head.

II. **Causes.**—Here four things are separately and progressively explained:—(1) Why there are tides at all; (2) why there are two tides in twenty-four hours; (3) why the spring-tides rise higher, and (4) why the neap-tides fall lower, than the usual or average tides. In explaining these points, either models or diagrams should be used. The teacher will do well to copy on the black-board the diagrams illustrating this subject in the text-book of "Physical Geography."

III. **The Tide-Wave.**—Two points are noted regarding this;—(1) Its *course*, which is traced from its origin in the Antarctic Ocean to the coast of England; (2) its *velocity*, with special reference to the occurrence of "bores." In connection with both points, constant reference should be made to the map.

MODEL LESSON: FORM OF THE EARTH.

Articles required.—*A Globe or a Map of the World in hemispheres: an Orange.*

INTRODUCTION.—Tell that people once thought that the Earth was flat, and that for a great many years hardly any one would believe those learned men who had discovered that it was round.

HEADS.	MATTER.	METHOD.
DEFINITION.	The Earth is round like an orange.	Explain that the Earth is slightly flattened at two opposite points called the Poles, and that it bulges out at the middle or Equator.
PROOFS.	1. **Ships at Sea.**—When a ship comes in sight, first the topmasts and the rigging are seen, and last of all the hull.	Show that if the surface of the sea were not curved, but a watery plain, we should see the whole ship at once.
	2. **Mountains seen from a distance.**—The tops of mountains are seen long before the land at their bases.	Illustrate by the fact that the peaks of the Himalaya Mountains may be seen from a distance of 200 miles.
	3. **Voyages round the Earth.**—Ships have sailed round the Earth, and have reached the port from which they started without changing their course.	Show on map Magellan's first voyage round the world—from Spain—westerly course—3 years 29 days—1519-1522. First Englishman who sailed round the world, Sir Francis Drake—1577-1580.
	4. **The Sun rising at different times.**—As we travel eastward the sun rises earlier; as we travel westward it rises later. This shows that the Earth is round from east to west.	Illustrate by stating that a telegram sent from Ireland at 2 o'clock on Friday afternoon reaches New York at half-past 9 *the same morning*.
	5. **The Stars.**—As we travel north or south new stars come into view, while those behind us disappear below the horizon. This shows that the Earth is round from north to south	Show that this fact also proves that the Earth moves round from east to west. If it moved from north to south, all the stars would be visible in turn, according to the position of the Earth in its orbit.
	6. **The Shadow of the Earth.**—In eclipses of the moon the shadow of the Earth on the moon is always circular . . .	Illustrate by the reflection of an object in a looking-glass, or by the shadow of an object on a wall.

MODEL LESSON: A MAP.

Articles required.—*A Globe or an Orange—Map of the World—Map of Europe—Map of England.*

INTRODUCTION.—Show a picture— Explain the use of pictures in representing scenes in other lands, &c.

HEADS.	MATTER.	METHOD.
DEFINITION.	A map is a drawing of the world, or of any portion of it, to show the position of places on its surface.	Explain that a map gives a kind of bird's-eye view, as seen from above. Sketch the school, and draw a plan of the school—compare picture with plan. Show map of World, and point out England — show map of Europe, and point out England—show map of England.
DIRECTIONS.	Top: the north. Bottom: the south. Right hand: the east. Left hand: the west.	Make diagram, thus:— N W + E S Show the use of these points in noting directions. Show how to find the four points by observing the position of the sun at noon.
LINES.	Lines of Latitude: running from east to west, parallel to the Equator. Lines of Longitude: running from north to south.	Make a diagram of a globe, showing lines of latitude and longitude. Explain their use in marking the exact position of places.
GENERAL FEATURES.	Coast: shown by wavy lines which surround the land... Mountains: shown by shaded or thick lines which run on the land........... Rivers: shown by wavy lines which run from the interior to the coast.......... Towns: shown by dots......	Draw coast line of England. Draw mountains. Draw rivers. Mark towns.
USES.	To teach geography....... To show the position of places To show the comparative size of countries, seas, &c. .... To show the directions of mountains, rivers, &c.	Illustrate by present lesson. Illustrate by several examples. Compare two countries on same map. Illustrate by several examples.

MODEL LESSON: CLIMATE.

INTRODUCTION.—When we are going on a journey, why do we look anxiously at the sky? To see if the weather be suitable. Show that the weather depends on climate.

HEADS.	MATTER.	METHOD.
DEFINITION.	Climate is the prevailing temperature and moisture of any given place.	Ask questions respecting climate of place in which school is situated
CAUSES OF CHANGE.	Latitude.—The nearer a country is to the equator the hotter it is; the farther it is away the colder it is......	Show relative positions of Earth and Sun, and how the equator receives more of the Sun's rays than any other part of the Earth.
	Elevation.—The higher a place is above the sea-level the colder it is............	Show that even in hot countries the tops of high mountains are covered with snow; for example, Chimborazo, close to the equator, in South America.
	Aspect.—Lands which slope toward the equator receive more heat than those which slope toward the poles....	Explain that the former receive more of the sun's rays than the latter.
	Nearness to the sea.—Places near the sea are neither so cold in winter nor so hot in summer as places far removed from it.........	Explain that water reduces the heat of summer and the cold of winter, because it remains longer cool, and longer warm, than land. Compare Riga (winter temp. 22°, summer 63°) with Moscow (winter 11°, summer 67°).
	Direction of mountain ranges.—Mountains afford shelter from cold winds.......	Examples: north of Europe (protected); north of Asia (unprotected).
	Character of soil.—Rocky and sandy soil is hot; moist and forest land is cool.......	Show that soils differ in their power of acquiring and retaining heat.
	Cultivation of soil.—As forests are cleared and the land is drained, the climate of a country becomes drier and warmer	Illustrate this by referring to North America.
	Prevailing winds.—Sea winds are moist and refreshing; land winds are dry and enervating.............	Compare the effects of the west wind and the east wind on the British Isles.
	Ocean currents.—Sea winds are affected by ocean currents, some of which are warm and others cold....	Refer to the Gulf Stream and the Labrador Current.

MODEL LESSON: TIDES.

INTRODUCTION.—If any of the children have been to the sea-side, ask them why they were sometimes unable to continue their sports on the sands. The tide covered the sands.

HEADS.	MATTER.	METHOD.
DEFINITION.	Tides are the alternate rising and falling of the waters of the ocean. The highest point is called *high water;* the lowest point, *low water.*	Explain *alternate;* also connect the words *flow* and *ebb* with *high water* and *low water.*
CAUSES.	**Of Tides in General.**—Tides are caused by the attraction of the moon, modified by the attraction of the sun. **Of Two Tides in 24 Hours.**—The attraction of the moon draws the waters from the earth; but the moon also draws the solid earth towards it, so that the waters stand out on the opposite side. **Of Spring Tides.**—At new and at full moon the attraction of the sun acts in the same line as that of the moon, and then the tide is higher than usual. **Of Neap Tides.**—At the moon's first and third quarters, the line of its action is at right angles with that of the sun's action, and then the tide is lower than usual.	Children will understand these explanations much better if diagrams are drawn on the black-board. The spring tides and the neap tides cannot be understood fully without some such assistance. For diagrams, see "Physical Geography" (Royal School Series), p. 17.
THE TIDE-WAVE.	**Its Course.**—It rises in the Antarctic Ocean, and a branch sweeps up each of the three great oceans,—Pacific, Atlantic, and Indian. The Atlantic tide advances northward at a steady pace. Thirty hours after leaving the Antarctic Ocean it reaches the west of England . . . . . **Its Velocity.**—The narrower the channel through which the tide-wave flows, the higher does it rise and the greater is its velocity. In some parts it travels at the rate of 1,000 miles an hour, and rises to a height of 50 or 60 feet	Show course on map of World. Give instances: Bristol Channel, Bay of Fundy, and the Ganges. Explain that in these instances the tide-wave is called a "bore." Describe its appearance and action.

EXERCISES.
Matter for Notes of Lessons.

THE SEASONS.

The divisions of the year according to the distribution of heat and cold—spring is the seed-sowing time, when plants begin to vegetate; summer is the hottest period of the year, when days are long and vegetation is most luxuriant; autumn is the harvest time, when plants begin to die and trees to shed their leaves; winter is the coldest period of the year, when days are short and vegetation stops—the cause of the change of seasons is the slanting axis of the Earth, which brings its northern part more directly under the sun's rays at one period of the year, and the southern part at another.

A RIVER.

A stream of water flowing over the land—the basin is the whole district drained by a river and its tributaries—the water-shed is the ridge of land which separates the basins of two or more rivers—the source is the commencement; it may be in a spring, a lake, a glacier, &c.—the bed or channel is the hollow worn out by the stream—the right and left banks are the sides of the channel—the slope is the incline of the bed of the river toward the sea; some rivers rise at great elevations—the velocity or speed of the current depends on the slope—rapids, water-falls, cascades, and cataracts, are caused by peculiar formations in the bed of the river—the course, whether straight or winding, depends on the slope—the volume or quantity of water which a river contains depends on the character of the country through which it flows—tributaries or feeders are streams that flow into larger ones—the confluence is where two streams unite—the mouth is where the river enters the sea—the delta is the land enclosed between the extreme mouths of a river—the estuary is that part of a river that is affected by the tide.

WINDS.

Currents of air—chief causes of wind are change of temperature, and the Earth's rotation—the rate of wind varies from five miles an hour to one hundred miles an hour—five miles an hour is called a light breeze; thirty to forty miles an hour, a gale; fifty miles, a storm; eighty to one hundred miles, a hurricane—winds vary in their direction and nature; there are constant winds, variable winds, periodical winds, and local winds—the principal constant winds are the trade winds—variable winds, the doldrums, &c.—periodical winds, the monsoons of the Indian Ocean, and the land and sea breezes of tropical countries—local winds, simoom, a dry, noxious desert wind in Arabia, called by the Turks samiel; harmattan, the desert wind of Western Africa, also called the sirocco (*in Italy*), and the solano (*in Spain*); typhoons, the hurricanes of the China Sea; cyclones, the hurricanes of the Indian Ocean and the West India seas; pamperos, the south-west winds from the pampas of South America; etesian winds, north-east winds which blow across the Mediterranean towards Africa.

ADDITIONAL SUBJECTS:—

The Atmosphere.	Oceans.	Motions of the Earth.
River Basins.	Mountains.	The Moon.
Glaciers.	Waves.	Man.
Icebergs.	Currents.	Plant Life.
Continents.	The Zones.	Animal Life.

DOMESTIC ECONOMY.

CHAPTER XII.

NOTES OF LESSONS ON DOMESTIC ECONOMY.

Domestic Economy, or Household Management, as it might more simply be called, has lately assumed a prominent place, especially in the education of girls. It would be difficult to exaggerate the importance of the subject in respect of what it teaches; and the fact that it has practical bearings on the work of life does not make the study less valuable as a means of exercising and training the mind. One of the chief advantages of the subject is, that it gives the teacher an opportunity of imparting a good deal of scientific knowledge in a popular form and in a practical connection. The uses and the qualities of food, for example, cannot be understood without some knowledge of physiology; while some acquaintance with chemistry is necessary in order to understand the principles of its preparation. It should be the aim of thoughtful teachers to keep in view both the theoretical and the practical applications of the subject, both when they are preparing their notes and while giving their lessons.

The subjects selected for the Model Lessons in this chapter are, first, a material substance—Food; and, secondly, a process or system—Ventilation. Most of the subjects prescribed in domestic economy will be found adaptable either to the one or to the other of these tables, with slight modifications. Clothing, drink, and dwellings, correspond with food, and may be treated in nearly the same way; cooking, digestion, and the circulation of the blood, will follow the plan of the lesson on ventilation.

1. FOOD.

The Notes of the Lesson on Food are arranged under these heads :—

    I. Definition.
    II. Kinds.
    III. Sources.
    IV. Preparation.
    V. Uses.

I. **Definition.**—This should not be a mere dictionary meaning of the word, but should describe briefly the essential function of the thing. It is not enough to say that food is that which we feed on, or that which we eat. The definition must refer to the work done by food in nourishing the body and in repairing its waste.

II. **Kinds.**—The kinds of food are described with respect to function—warmth-giving, flesh-forming, and bone-making. The constituent elements of each kind of food are also given; and in the " method " examples are added.

III. **Sources.**—These are arranged under the "three kingdoms of Nature," as they are called, the vegetable, the animal, and the mineral. Examples of each kind of food should be asked for; and attention should be called to the wide range whence man draws his supplies.

IV. **Preparation.**—Under this head the different methods of cooking food are mentioned—roasting, boiling, broiling, &c. The " method " here includes a description of the several processes, particular notice being taken of the effect of each process on the nutritive properties of the food.

V. **Uses.**—This head describes in detail, and in the form of effects, what is stated in general terms in the " definition " as the function of food. It also reflects what is said under the second head regarding the kinds of food; for the three main uses of food are, to give warmth, to form flesh, and to make bone. The " method " suggests illustrations and comparisons by which the use of food, and the work done by food, may be made clear to he young.

It may be necessary to repeat here what has been said in other chapters, that the whole of the material in this table need not be used in a single lesson. It will depend on the age and stage of the scholars how far detail should be gone into, and therefore how many lessons the matter shall occupy.

2. VENTILATION.

The heads in this and similar cases are the following :—

    I. Definition.
    II. Object.
    III. Methods.
    IV. Results.

I. **Definition.**—In connection with this it will be necessary to describe the composition of pure air, and to show how it is made impure or is spoiled. Having been spoiled, and made unwholesome, it is necessary to get rid of it, and to introduce fresh air in its place. That is the work of ventilation.

II. **Object.**—The ultimate object is what is here referred to—namely, to preserve health; not the object stated in the "definition," which is, to keep up a supply of pure air. The "method" refers to the effects of air on health.

III. **Methods.**—This is the most important head in the lesson. It enumerates and describes the different contrivances adopted for the purpose of changing the air in dwellings. It should of course be explained in connection with these, that they all aim at the production of a current, or of circulation; and that this is effected by taking advantage of the different densities of warm and of cold air.

IV. **Results.**—As in the former case, this head in effect repeats the "definition" and the "object" in another form. It affords an opportunity, however, of showing what are the evils which a good system of ventilation prevents, and thus also of urging the great importance of attending to the subject both in theory and in practice.

NOTES OF LESSONS ON DOMESTIC ECONOMY. 103

MODEL LESSON: FOOD.

HEADS.	MATTER.	METHOD.
DEFINITION.	That which supports life, and repairs the waste of the body.	Show that without food the body wastes away, and at last dies. Show that appetite tells us when we require food.
KINDS.	**Warmth-giving.**—Those that contain (1) starch, (2) fat, and (3) sugar. **Flesh-forming.**—Those that contain (1) fibrine, (2) gluten, (3) albumen, (4) casein, (5) gelatine. **Bone-making.**—Those that contain mineral properties.	Examples—(1) wheat, potatoes, (2) flesh, (3) beetroot. Ex.—(1) flesh, (2) outer husks of grain plants, (3) eggs, (4) milk, (5) fish. Ex.—salt; soda, found in fresh vegetables.
SOURCES.	**Vegetable.**—Grain-plants, roots, fruits, leaves, farina, sugar. **Animal.**—Meat, fish, game, poultry, cheese, eggs, milk, butter. **Mineral.**—Salt.	Show that man has made all the kingdoms of nature contribute to the supply of his wants. Ask for examples of each kind of food, naming whence they are got.
PREPARATION.	**Roasting.**—Cooking before a fire. **Boiling.**—Cooking in boiling water. **Broiling.**—Cooking over a fire on a gridiron. **Baking.**—Cooking in an oven. **Frying.**—Cooking over a fire in a shallow pan. **Stewing.**—Cooking in water not allowed to boil.	Explain the different processes. Show that those should be preferred which present the food in its most wholesome form, and which at the same time cause least waste of its nutritious properties. Show that stewing best fulfils these conditions.
USES.	Keeps up a uniform heat in the body.	Show that food supplies solid fuel to make warmth, and moisture to cool superfluous heat.
	Supplies force.	Compare with steam-engine, which cannot move till it be supplied with the power which is stored up in coal.
	Makes flesh and tissue.	Show that the body is subject to daily waste, which is supplied by our food.
	Supplies material for bones and joints.	Compare with iron joints, which soon wear out, while ours are renewed by our food.

MODEL LESSON: VENTILATION.

HEADS.	MATTER.	METHOD.
DEFINITION.	The process of keeping up a constant supply of pure air in dwellings.	Show the various ways in which air becomes impure or spoiled.
OBJECT.	To preserve health.	Show that pure air is as necessary to health as pure water and wholesome food. Air once breathed is poisonous. Refer to Black Hole of Calcutta.
METHODS.	**The chimney valve.**—A valve let into the chimney near the ceiling of the room. It is self-acting. It opens so as to carry the foul air into the chimney, without admitting an inward draught. **India-rubber tubes.**—Pipes, one end of which is carried through the wall into the open air, and the other is deposited near the fire-place. They cause a constant change of air—the cold air forcing out the warm. **Perforated zinc tubes.**—These tubes are carried close to the ceiling from outer wall to outer wall. They are open at the ends. They carry off foul air, and admit fresh in tiny streams. **Perforated plates.**—Boxes fixed into the wall, each having on the outside a perforated plate, and on the inside a trap door. **Windows.**—The opening of windows is generally sufficient to ventilate small rooms.	Explain the general principle on which nature works to procure ventilation,—namely, the production of currents, by the heavy cold air rushing down and displacing the warm air, which is light. Show that, in order to make ventilation thorough, it is necessary not only to admit fresh air, but also to provide for the escape of impure air. This is often done by opening a window both at the top and at the bottom. The warm air, being the lighter, escapes at the top opening, and the fresh air enters at the bottom.
RESULTS.	Healthy houses. . . . . Our comfort is increased. . . .	Show how ventilation carries off noxious vapours, which arise from drains, gas pipes, and dirty rooms. It may thus prevent fevers, &c. Describe the uncomfortable feeling occasioned by close, hot rooms, and show that fresh air may be enjoyed by all who are willing to admit it into their houses.

EXERCISES.

Matter for Notes of Lessons.

CLOTHING.

The covering of the body—cotton, woollen, linen, silk, skins—from animal and vegetable sources—preparation of material by spinning and weaving; of articles of clothing by cutting out and sewing—clothing keeps in the natural heat of the body; keeps cold from reaching the body; improves our appearance—we should dress according to our circumstances; neatly; with a due regard to the state of the weather.

DWELLINGS.

Places for sheltering mankind in families—tents, huts, cottages, houses, halls, mansions, palaces, &c.—materials, stone, brick, wood, iron, concrete, slate, mud, straw, &c.—houses should have healthy sites, well-built walls, thoroughly ventilated rooms, good drainage, be well supplied with pure water—they are to shelter man from cold and wet; to shield him from the rays of the sun; to enable families to live together in privacy; to secure the safety of property.

SAVING OR THRIFT.

Laying by money—to keep money for some special purpose, or to have it when unable to earn it—clothing and coal clubs are to enable the poor to save sufficient in summer to assist them in winter—benefit or friendly societies are to provide a fund out of which a weekly amount is paid to sick members, and also a sum of money to the relatives when a member dies—penny-banks are established in connection with most schools, to enable the children to make small deposits on their own or their parents' account—the post-office savings-bank receives small sums, and there is government security for the money—banks pay interest on the money deposited; being the possessor of money gives a man a feeling of independence, secures him attention in sickness, and comfort in old age.

ADDITIONAL SUBJECTS:—
Marketing.	Washing.	Division of Labour.
Cleaning.	Drink.	Health.

MORALS.

CHAPTER XIII

NOTES OF LESSONS ON MORALS.

A SYSTEMATIC lesson on a moral subject—a duty, a virtue, a vice—will sometimes be suggested by the reading lesson of the day, especially if its subject be a story, an anecdote, or an incident in history. Whether the moral lesson originate in this way or not, use should be made of illustrative stories in connection with it as often as possible. Children are more readily interested in and impressed with any subject when it is presented to them in a concrete form. The chief difficulty in the way of giving such lessons is their abstract character; and this difficulty cannot be obviated except in the way indicated.

Moral lessons of the kind sketched in this chapter belong, of course, to the most advanced classes. Apart from the mental exercise involved, there is an important advantage in accustoming pupil-teachers and the older scholars to reflect seriously on questions bearing on duty and the rules of conduct.

The Notes of the lessons on this subject are arranged as follows:-

    I. DEFINITION.
    II. PERSONS.
    III. MOTIVES.
    IV. MANNER.
    V. EFFECTS.

I. **Definition.**—This is intended to give, in a few simple words, an explanation of the virtue or principle to be dealt with in the lesson. Here it will be advantageous to make use at once of contrasts and of concrete examples.

II. **Persons.**—Under this head we answer the question, Whom ought we to obey, be grateful to, forgive? &c. Obedience should be given to those in authority over us; gratitude should be shown to our benefactors; forgiveness to our enemies; politeness to all.

III. **Motives.**—This answers the question, Why ought we to perform a certain duty—to be obedient, polite, grateful, forgiving? The answer might be given, in almost every case, " Because it is our duty." But that is not enough. We must try to show why it is our duty, or at least to suggest some considerations which will appeal to the minds of children as adequate to enforce the duty.

IV. **Manner.**—This answers the question, How should the particular duty be performed? Every one knows that the right thing may be done in a wrong way: we may obey in a sulky and tardy manner; we may forgive in an ungracious way. The manner in which an action is done may either impair or enhance its value, and it is therefore important that notice should be taken of this in every case.

V. **Effects.**—These may have regard either to ourselves or to others, or to both. It is not always easy to distinguish between motives and effects. If the effects of an action are likely to be good, that is certainly a motive for doing it; but care must be taken not to represent the good effects which an action may bring to the doer of it as a right motive in his case. In short, motives of a purely selfish kind ought to be discouraged; and therefore the results of our conduct to ourselves should be stated as " effects " rather than " motives."

It should be observed that all the subjects which may be taken up under the name of " Morals " are not susceptible of the same treatment or method of classification. The Model Lesson and the Comparative Table show that the plan is capable of wide application; but all the examples given in the Exercises will not come under the same arrangement of heads.

MODEL LESSON: OBEDIENCE.

INTRODUCTION.—Tell a story of an obedient child.

HEADS.	MATTER.	METHOD.
DEFINITION.	Doing what we are told to do.	Show that some children attend to what is said to them; others do not.
PERSONS.	Those in authority over us:— Our **Heavenly Father**, God, whose commandments we find in the Bible .... Our **Parents**, whom God commands us to obey .... Our **Teachers**, who have charge of us at school .... Our **Masters**, who employ us. Our **Rulers**, the Queen and those appointed by her to assist in the government of the country	Show what is meant by "authority," and that every one is subject to a higher power. Explain the different kinds of relationship which exist, between the creature and the Creator, children and parents, scholars and teachers, servants and masters, subjects and rulers.
MOTIVES.	It is our duty............ Those who are placed over us know what is best for us .. They have our welfare at heart. They are responsible to others for our training.........	Explain that we owe obedience to Him who made us, and to those who rear us, teach us, employ us, and rule over us. Show that this is the result of experience. Illustrate by instances of self-sacrifice. Show that teachers are responsible to parents, parents to rulers, all to God.
MANNER.	**Promptly**: as soon as we can after receiving the command. **Cheerfully**: willingly and gladly; without grumbling. **Without Question**: not stopping to ask why the order has been given	Show that the more quickly a command is obeyed the easier it is. Explain that obedience should be regarded as a pleasure. Show that children could not always understand the reason.
EFFECTS.	**Approbation**: we shall have the good opinion of those whom we have obeyed .... **Happiness**: we have done our duty, and have nothing to be sorry for .... **Good Order**: in the family, in the school, in society	Compare praise and blame, rewards and punishments. Illustrate by describing the feelings of a disobedient child. Contrast a family in which the children are obedient with one in which they are the reverse.

COMPARISON OF MORAL SUBJECTS.

Arrangement of Lesson.	POLITENESS.	GRATITUDE.	FORGIVENESS.
DEFINITION.	Good manners—considering others before ourselves.	A feeling of thankfulness for kindness received.	Pardoning those who have done us any injury.
PERSONS.	To all with whom we have to do: our parents—our brothers and sisters—our friends—our superiors, inferiors, equals.	To those from whom we have received any benefit: God—our parents—our teachers—our friends.	To those who offend or harm us, whether by accident or intentionally.
MOTIVES.	It makes life more agreeable—it gains us the respect of others.	It shows that we appreciate the kindness we have received.	It is our duty: Jesus said, "Love your enemies"—we wish to be forgiven: in the Lord's Prayer we are taught to say, "Forgive us our debts, as we forgive our debtors."
MANNER.	We treat one another with respect—we say "please," and "thank you"—we give up our own comforts and pleasures—we avoid giving trouble—we avoid saying or doing anything that may hurt another's feelings.	By word—by act, in returning kindness for kindness, and in doing kindnesses to others.	Freely, with the whole heart—promptly, at once—cheerfully, with kindness.
EFFECTS.	We add to one another's comfort—others are polite to us.	We are united to one another by bonds of love—it leads to future kindnesses.	Enemies become friends—our characters are improved—others forgive us—we may ask God to forgive us our sins.

EXERCISES—MORALS, &c.

Matter for Notes of Lessons to be arranged on the plan of the Model Lesson.

CRUELTY TO ANIMALS.

It is cowardly; animals are often helpless in our hands, and unable either to plead their own cause or to defend themselves—it is unjust; God has placed them under our dominion, and we have no right to abuse the confidence placed in us by oppressing creatures of a lower order than ourselves—it is ungrateful; but for the lower animals our lot would be less comfortable, they are our benefactors—it is debasing; it hardens our own hearts.

PUNCTUALITY.

Being at the proper place, or engaged in the proper work at the right time—it gives us time for our work; we do not require to hurry, and the work is better done—it saves the time of others; while they were waiting for us, they might have been occupied in some useful work—it causes us to be regarded as trustworthy; if we are careless about our time, people will refuse to trust us, for they will <u>think</u> that our work is sure to be neglected.

WAR.

It arouses angry feelings; nations previously at peace, and regarding each other with friendly feelings, are caused to look upon each other as enemies—it sacrifices life; numbers are slain, or die from exposure, famine, fatigue, &c.—it destroys property; towns are plundered and burned, crops are trampled down, or left untended—it causes much suffering; men are wounded, or sickness is brought on, widows and orphans are left to struggle through the world without a husband's or a father's help or care—it costs vast sums of money; arms and ammunition have to be supplied, a large army has to be fed and clothed, means of transport have to be provided, damage caused by the war has to be made good.

ADDITIONAL SUBJECTS:—

Temperance.	Cleanliness.	Honesty.
Charity.	Truthfulness.	Forbearance.
Tidiness.	Patience.	Thrift.

SCRIPTURE.

CHAPTER XIV.

NOTES OF LESSONS ON SCRIPTURE.

The Historical and Biographical lessons from the Bible may be treated in the same way, and under the same heads, as the similar lessons on English History. (See chapter IX.) There are, however, two classes of Scripture lessons which require special treatment, and which admit of convenient and instructive sub-division. These are the Parables and the Miracles of our Lord.

1. A PARABLE.

The notes of a lesson on a Parable should be arranged under these heads :—
I. Place.
II. Occasion.
III. Subject.
IV. Explanation.
V. Lessons.

I. **Place.**—This should not only name the town or village in which the parable was spoken, but as often as possible it should suggest the whole scene. Thus, in the Model Lesson on "The Sower," it is stated that it was spoken at Capernaum, and near the Sea of Galilee. The value of this is seen under the third head, where it is said that Jesus is supposed to have had the parable suggested to him by seeing a man sowing seed on a field near the Sea of Galilee.

II. **Occasion.**—This is different from the place and scene of the parable. It includes the circumstances which led Jesus to speak it, or in the midst of which it emerged.

III. **Subject.**—This indicates the subject of the story as a story, and without reference to its inner meaning, which belongs to the next head.

IV. **Explanation.**—This is the most important head of the lesson. It shows the meaning of the story. It explains for what each person or thing in the story stands in the spiritual application of it. Thus, in the parable of the Sower, the sower himself is interpreted to signify the preacher, while the seed is the word of God, and the soil is the hearts of men. In the "method" of this part of the lesson, the object should be to bring out the points of resemblance between the things compared. The questions to be answered are such as these:—In what respect is a preacher like a sower? Why may the word of God be compared to seed, and the hearts of men to soil? In answering the latter question care should be taken to trace the resemblance in the details mentioned under each subject,— to show the spiritual significance of the *wayside, stony places,* &c.; and of the seed *devoured by fowls, scorched by the sun, choked by thorns,* and *that brought forth good fruit.*

V. **Lessons.**—Reflections and practical applications arising out of the parable are given under this head.

2. A MIRACLE.

The heads most suitable for a lesson on a Miracle are the following:—

    I. SCENE.
    II. DETAILS.
    III. RESULTS.
    IV. LESSONS.

I. **Scene.**—The first thing to be noted under this head is the place where the miracle was wrought; but to this there should be added, when the material for it exists, a description of the surrounding circumstances. Thus, in the lesson on "The Cripple Healed," it is first mentioned that the miracle occurred at the Pool of Bethesda; but, in order fully to realize the scene, note must be taken of the situation of the pool, near the sheep-market; and of the surrounding porches crowded with sick persons, eagerly watching for the moving of the water.

II. **Details.**—This is the most important head. It narrates in order the whole doings and sayings of Jesus in connection with the event. The aim should be to place the details as vividly as possible before the class, and so arranged that they may be easily remembered and readily reproduced. This object will be materially helped by giving prominence to the salient points, as suggested in the "method" of the Model Lesson; and by grouping the other incidents around these.

III. **Results.**—Under this head there are included both the immediate issue of the miracle and its effect on those who witnessed or who heard of it. Thus, in "The Cripple Healed," it is stated that (1) immediately the man was made whole; and that (2) he took up his bed and walked. These particulars relate to the cripple and his healing; but a third particular is added, showing the effect of the miracle on the Jews, and its consequence to Jesus—Jesus was persecuted by the Jews. In "The Sick of the Palsy" two results are mentioned, the one relating to the subject of the miracle, the other to the onlookers: —(1) the man was healed; (2) the multitudes marvelled and glorified God.

IV. **Lessons.**—Under this head are mentioned practical reflections, similar to those drawn from the parable. In connection with these lessons, it may be useful to refer to texts of Scripture which either embody or illustrate their teaching, as is done in the "method" column of the Model Lesson on "The Cripple Healed."

It will be found easy to adapt the heads given in the Model Lessons to any of the parables or miracles. Examples of this are given in the Comparative tables.

MODEL LESSON: THE SOWER.

Matthew xiii.; *Mark* iv.; *Luke* viii.

INTRODUCTION.—Read the parable, or hear it read by the class.

HEADS.	MATTER.	METHOD.
PLACE.	Capernaum, near the Sea of Galilee.	Show on map.
OCCASION.	The gathering together of multitudes to see and to hear Jesus.	Refer to the desire to see the wonderful things done by Jesus.
SUBJECT.	A man sowing seed in a field.	Our Saviour is supposed to have seen some person sowing seed near the Sea of Galilee, to whom he directed his hearers' attention.
EXPLANATION.	1. **The sower**: a preacher.	Show that both look to the future for results.
	2. **The ground**: the hearts of men.	Both need culture, and receive seed, and bring forth fruit.
	(1.) *Way side*: hearts hardened by sin.	Compare hardened hearts with a beaten footpath.
	(2.) *Stony places*: hearts unable to retain the seed for want of faith.	Compare want of faith with want of soil.
	(3.) *Among thorns*: hearts occupied by cares and pleasures.	Compare cares and pleasures with thorns.
	(4.) *Good ground*: hearts made willing to receive the truth.	Compare with good soil.
	3. **The seed**: the word of God.	Show that the end of both is to produce new life, yielding fruit.
	(1.) *Devoured by fowls*: stolen by Satan.	Explain how Satan acts on the heart.
	(2.) *Scorched by the sun*: subjected to tribulation or persecution.	Refer to persons who shrink back from fear of others, and to renegades in times of persecution.
	(3.) *Choked by thorns*: the good overcome by the evil.	Show force of comparison.
	(4.) *Brought forth good fruit*: resulted in a holy, useful life.	Refer to Matt. xiii. 23.
LESSONS.	1. The state of our hearts while hearing the truth is of very great importance.	Show that if the heart does not receive the teaching, all is of no effect.
	2. The enemies we have to contend with are Satan, the world, our own evil hearts.	Show that if the heart be right toward God, the world and Satan cannot prevail.

NOTES OF LESSONS ON SCRIPTURE. 115

COMPARISON OF PARABLES.

Arrangement of Lesson.	THE PEARL.	THE LOST SHEEP.	THE TRUE VINE.
RECORDED.	Matthew xiii.	Matthew xviii.; Luke xv.	John xv.
PLACE.	Capernaum, near to the Sea of Galilee.	Galilee.	Jerusalem.
OCCASION.	The gathering together of a great multitude to see and hear Jesus.	When replying to disciples, who had asked, "Who is the greatest in the kingdom of heaven?"	To the disciples, after the Last Supper.
SUBJECT.	A man seeking pearls, and finding one of great price, sold all that he had and bought it.	A shepherd's joy on finding a lost sheep.	The living union of a vine and its branches.
EXPLANATION.	A merchantman: a seeker of the truth. Pearls: the truth. Pearl of great price: Christ. Sold all: gave up all his possessions to obtain it.	The shepherd: Jesus. The sheep: mankind. The lost sheep: those who are living without Christ. His joy: Christ rejoices over every sinner that repenteth.	The vine: Christ. The branches: all true believers. The husbandman: the Father. The fruit: a holy and useful life.
LESSONS.	1. Earnest seekers are rewarded. 2. There is but one pearl of great price. 3. All must be given up, if needful, to obtain Christ.	1. Man cannot save himself. 2. Christ is the only Saviour. 3. God has no pleasure in the death of a sinner.	1. Every believer must have a living union with Christ. 2. Holiness grows through this union with him. 3. We live in him; and through him we "bring forth fruit unto God."

EXERCISES—PARABLES.

Matter for Notes of Lessons to be arranged on the plan of the Model Lesson.

THE TARES.
MATTHEW xiii.

Capernaum—the gathering together of multitudes to hear Jesus—an enemy sowing tares among wheat—the sower of the good seed, the Son of man; the field, the world; the good seed, converted persons; the tares, unconverted persons; the enemy, the devil; the harvest, the end of the world; the reapers, the angels—the good and the bad are mixed in this world; at the end of the world there will be a final separation of the good from the bad.

THE LABOURERS.
MATTHEW xx.

Perea—in reply to Peter's question, "Behold, we have forsaken all, and followed thee; what shall we have therefore?"—the engagement and payment of labourers in a vineyard—the householder, God; the vineyard, the Church of Christ; the labourers, members of Christ's Church; a penny a day, equal benefits to all; third, sixth, and ninth hours, the different periods of life arrived at before entering God's service—the labourers were not compelled to enter the householder's service, so we may refuse to enter God's service; we must not delay our acceptance of God's offered mercy because some were called at the eleventh hour; they went as soon as called, and so must we, if we do not wish to risk our final acceptance.

THE WICKED HUSBANDMEN.
MATTHEW xxi.; MARK xii.; LUKE xx.

Jerusalem—in the temple, in reply to the chief priests and the elders of the people, who asked Jesus by what authority he taught—the treatment of the servants and the heir of the owner of a vineyard, by those to whom it had been let—the householder, God; the vineyard, the Church; the husbandmen, the Jews; the servants, the prophets, whom the Jews persecuted; the heir, Jesus Christ—man may persecute God's servants and oppose his Church, but he cannot destroy it; those who reject the Son of God will be punished.

MODEL LESSON: THE CRIPPLE HEALED.
John V.

INTRODUCTION.—Describe a feast of the Jews. Show that at the three great annual feasts—Passover, Pentecost, and Tabernacles—all the males of the nation were commanded to go up to Jerusalem. Describe the family gatherings, the crowded streets, the services, &c.

HEADS.	MATTER.	METHOD.
SCENE.	The Pool of Bethesda....	Explain Bethesda, "the house of mercy." Describe the arrangement of the pool, with steps and porches.
	Near the sheep-market..	Describe the walls of Jerusalem — entered by gates —gates had different names —this called the sheep-gate —sheep taken through it for sacrifice at the temple.
	The porches in which lay the impotent folk....	Describe the waiting crowd and how anxiously they and their friends watched the waters of the pool.
	The healing water....	Show that only one could be healed each time the angel came. This caused many to wait a long time without being healed.
DETAILS.	Jesus visited the pool—saw the cripple lying there— knew that he had been there a long time—asked him if he would be made whole — heard the man describe his friendless and helpless state—said to him, "Rise, take up thy bed, and walk"....	This portion of the lesson should be very vividly placed before the children. Show the man's helpless, friendless condition; thirty-eight years ill, and no one to put him into the pool. Bring out fully the man's need, and our Saviour's power and love.
RESULTS.	1. Immediately the man was made whole......	Show that the instantaneous cure proved the divine power of Jesus.
	2. He took up his bed, and walked...........	This was a proof of the man's restoration. Describe Eastern beds.
	3. Jesus was persecuted by the Jews..........	Healing the man on the Sabbath was made an excuse for finding fault with Jesus.
LESSONS.	1. Jesus is ready to help those who are in need ..	Refer to Matt. xi. 28.
	2. He knows all our wants before we tell him.....	Refer to Matt. vi. 8.

COMPARISON OF MIRACLES.

Arrangement of Lesson.	THE SICK OF THE PALSY.	THE CENTURION'S SERVANT.	THE WIDOW'S SON.
RECORDED.	*Matthew* ix.; *Mark* ii.; *Luke* v.	*Matthew* viii.; *Luke* vii.	*Luke* vii.
INTRODUCTION	Describe the multitude gathered to hear and see Jesus.	Describe the Roman occupation of Palestine.	Describe an Eastern funeral, &c.
SCENE.	Supposed to have been Simon Peter's house at Capernaum.	Capernaum, a town near the Sea of Galilee.	At the city gate of Nain, south of Mount Tabor.
DETAILS.	Jesus teaching in the house—healing the sick—the friends of the sick man unable to enter by the door, the crowd was so great—they went upon the roof and let the man down into the midst before Jesus—He saw their faith, and said to the man, "Thy sins be forgiven thee...... Arise, take up thy bed, and go unto thine house."	Jesus in Capernaum—centurion sent elders to Jesus—the centurion's request—our Lord's promise—the centurion's faith—Jesus commended his faith, and said, "Go thy way; and as thou hast believed, so be it done unto thee."	Jesus at the gate of the city—the funeral—the mourners—our Lord's compassion—His words to the widow, "Weep not."—He touched the bier, saying, "Young man, I say unto thee, Arise."
RESULTS.	1. The man was healed. 2. The multitudes marvelled, and glorified God.	The servant was healed in the self-same hour.	1. The young man sat up, and began to speak. 2. The people glorified God.
LESSON.	God rewards those who diligently seek Him.	The master's faith brought a blessing on his servant.	Jesus has compassion on those in trouble.

EXERCISES—MIRACLES.
Matter for Notes of Lessons to be arranged on the plan of the Model Lesson.

THE NOBLEMAN'S SON HEALED.
JOHN iv.

At Cana of Galilee—Jesus returned to Cana; a certain nobleman whose son was sick at Capernaum heard of this; he went unto Jesus and besought him to go to Capernaum, and heal his son; Jesus said, "Except ye see signs and wonders, ye will not believe;" the nobleman replied, "Sir, come down ere my child die;" Jesus said, "Go thy way; thy son liveth;" the nobleman believed, returned to his home, and found his son healed—in the same hour that Jesus spoke, the fever left the sick child; the nobleman and his whole house believed on Jesus—Christ's power is not limited by distance or place.

FIVE THOUSAND FED.
MATTHEW xiv.; MARK vi.; LUKE ix.; JOHN vi.

In Decapolis—Jesus had been followed by a great multitude into a desert place; he healed their sick; the disciples wished to send the people away to buy themselves food; Jesus said, "Give ye them to eat;" the disciples said that they had only five loaves, and two fishes; Jesus told them to arrange the people on the grass; the disciples did so; Jesus then blessed the food, and it was distributed among the people—five thousand men, besides women and children, were fed, and twelve basketfuls of fragments were gathered up; the people wished to make Jesus a king—if we seek first the kingdom of God and his righteousness, all other things shall be added.

TEN LEPERS CLEANSED.
LUKE xvii.

During one of Christ's journeys to Jerusalem—as he entered a certain village ten men stood afar off and cried, "Jesus, Master, have mercy on us;" he said, "Go shew yourselves unto the priests;" on their way they were cleansed; only one of them returned to thank Jesus; he was a Samaritan; Jesus said, "Were there not ten cleansed? but where are the nine? there are not found that returned to give glory to God, save this stranger;" then Jesus told the Samaritan his faith had made him whole—ten lepers were cleansed by the power of Jesus—we ought to thank God for his mercies.

APPLICATION.

CHAPTER XV.

GENERAL PRINCIPLES.

THOUGH as much variety as possible has been given to the Model Lessons in the preceding chapters, variety both of subject and of method of treatment, yet subjects may occur, both in examinations and in practice, to which none of these Models will exactly apply. What, in such a case, is the student advised to do?

No intelligent student can have studied the Model Lessons and worked the Exercises in this book, with any degree of care, without becoming familiar with the general principles which regulate the laying out of a lesson. It would be unreasonable to expect any student to remember the great variety of models given in these pages. They have not been given with that view, but rather for the purpose of affording practice, and of subjecting the mind to discipline, which will give facility and accuracy in the work of producing original schemes. It is believed that when a student has had the benefit of this practice and this discipline, he will experience no difficulty in putting his mind into the proper attitude for producing good work of the same kind.

From a comparison of the Model Lessons, it will be found that there are certain "heads" which occur very frequently. The following are some of these:—

DEFINITION.	EXAMPLE.	CLASS.	SOURCE.	RESULTS.
USES.	PROCESS.	MANNER.	PARTS.	KINDS.
QUALITIES.	LOCALITY.	HISTORY.	DETAILS.	HABITS.

GENERAL PRINCIPLES. 121

From their constant occurrence, such heads will become familiar, and will naturally take hold of the mind; and all that the student requires to do is to judge which of them will apply to any subject that is brought under his notice. The heads having been selected, they should be arranged in logical order.

An easily remembered principle, which will often suggest a good scheme of heads, is, that everything has a Beginning, a Middle, and an End. Several heads may correspond with each of these parts. For example :—

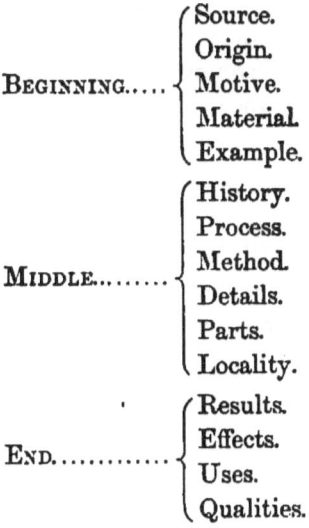

BEGINNING..... { Source. Origin. Motive. Material. Example.

MIDDLE......... { History. Process. Method. Details. Parts. Locality.

END............ { Results. Effects. Uses. Qualities.

This method will be found applicable to a large number of subjects.

Another plan, which will rarely fail to produce a workable scheme, is that of forming questions on the prescribed subject. The questions may be such as the following :—

1. What is it?
2. What is it like?
3. What is its use?
4. Of what is it made?
5. How is it made?
6. Where is it found?

In answer to these questions, we obtain the following heads respectively :—

    1. DEFINITION, OR CLASSIFICATION.
    2. DESCRIPTION, OR APPEARANCE.
    3. USE, OR OBJECT.
    4. MATERIAL.
    5. MANUFACTURE, OR PROCESS.
    6. LOCALITY, OR PLACE.

One or two examples will show how readily this principle may be applied. Let us suppose that we are asked to prepare notes of a lesson on a PLOUGH. We begin by asking ourselves as many questions about the plough as we can think of, such as,—

    1. What is a plough?
    2. What is it like?
    3. For what is it used?
    4. Of what is it made?
    5. Are there different kinds of ploughs?

Hence we get the following scheme, which, of course, might be much more fully worked out :—

A PLOUGH.

1. DEFINITION.	An implement of agriculture.
2. APPEARANCE AND PARTS.	Has a sharp point, for piercing the soil. A blade, or share, for turning up the soil. Shafts, for directing its course.
3. USE.	To turn over the soil before seed is sown.
4. MATERIAL.	Iron, steel, and wood.
5. KINDS.	Steam plough. Horse plough. Single plough. Double plough.

The method is equally applicable to an abstract subject, such as CHARITY. Here we ask,—

1. What is charity?
2. What is the opposite of charity?
3. Why should we show charity?
4. To whom should we show it?
5. How may we show it?
6. What are the effects of charity on ourselves and on others?

In answering these questions, we shall develop a scheme of which the following may be taken as an outline :—

CHARITY.

1. DEFINITION.	Acting kindly to others.
2. OPPOSITE.	Unkindness.
3. MOTIVES.	God's command. Regard for others. Self-respect.
4. OBJECTS, OR PERSONS.	All men, especially the poor and needy.
5. MANNER.	By gifts. By kind words. By judging in a kind spirit.
6. EFFECTS.	Happiness and comfort to others. Gratitude of those benefited. Satisfaction to ourselves.

In classes of very young children, the question mode is preferable to any other; and in that case questions may be substituted for the usual heads in the tables with very great advantage.

While it is necessary that every lesson should be complete, it is not desirable to multiply the number of heads, or of subdivisions of heads. In this matter, however, the teacher must be guided by the ages and the capacity of the scholars for whom his lesson is intended.

CONCLUSION.

ON GIVING A LESSON.

The questions discussed in the Introduction were, What are Notes of Lessons? and, In what does their value consist? In the subsequent chapters, forming the body of the work, we have shown how Notes of Lessons are made. It remains for us to make some remarks here, by way of practical application, on the use that should be made of prepared Notes in the act of Giving a Lesson.

In the first place, as little use as possible should be made of the written notes in the school-room. The chief purpose of the preparation of notes is to enable the teacher, while elaborating the scheme on paper, at the same time to master the scheme with his mind. An occasional reference to the notes, when minute details of fact and figure have to be gone into, is quite proper; but a slavish use of notes in presence of the class is very apt to destroy the confidence of the scholars in their teacher, and to deprive the lesson of life and spirit.

On the other hand, as much use as possible should be made of the black-board. On it the scheme of the lesson as it proceeds should be gradually worked out before the class. When the lesson is finished, the contents of the board should be an outline of the notes, and may be used with great effect in a recapitulation or review of the lesson. At the same time, great use should be made of maps, diagrams, illustrations, and models.

The most important point of all is, how the lesson should be given, by what method or methods the subject should be unfolded before the class. On this the interest and the value of the lesson essentially depend, and by his success in doing this part of his work the teacher's skill may best be appraised.

There are two methods in common use—the Expository and the Interrogative method; or more simply, lecturing and questioning. In the former, the teacher speaks, and the scholars listen, or are supposed to listen, to his exposition. In the latter, the teacher tries to find out what the children know, and to ascertain what they observe regarding an object placed before them.

There can be no doubt as to the relative value of these two methods, if each be used wholly by itself. In the matter of catching and retaining the interest of a class, there can be no comparison between them. Children who are merely lectured very soon become listless; their minds wander, and their attention flags. Children who are being questioned, whose knowledge is being drawn out, are kept constantly on the alert. Their minds are active; their eyes are eagerly fixed on the teacher, and their interest is lively and unmistakable.

In respect of their educational effect, the two methods bear the same relative value as they do as means of discipline; and for a similar reason. The mind is trained by being exercised. Thinking is an active, not a passive process. That method of teaching, therefore, will be most efficacious which is most successful in keeping the faculties of the children in a state of spontaneous activity; and there can be no doubt of the superiority of questioning over lecturing for that purpose. It is obvious, at the same time, that the most skilful questioning cannot extract from children what they do not know—cannot elicit information on an unknown subject. Direct instruction must therefore be to some extent combined with questioning; but the questioning method should occupy the chief place.

There should be no misunderstanding as to what kind of questioning is referred to. It is not the putting of formal questions for the purpose of receiving formal answers. It is not the use of a catechism, or anything approaching to that. It is the free and rapid conversational process by which teacher and scholars build up between them a little system of knowledge regarding a particular subject. Its aim is, first to elicit what the children know, and then to use that as a bridge to lead them to what is as yet unknown. This is sometimes called the Socratic* method of teaching. Its plan is to guide the scholars through a course of inquiry which begins in ignorance and ends in knowledge, which starts from error or misconception and arrives at truth. When a question is put which the scholars cannot answer, the teacher puts other questions relating to what they know, and thus leads them by a round-about road to the point which they failed to reach directly. The value of the process lies in the fact that the scholars make the discovery for themselves.

Let us take a simple example. Suppose, in the course of a lesson on the Lion, that the question is put—What is the use of its whiskers? The children cannot tell; and the following dialogue, or something like it, is carried on between the teacher and one scholar after another:—

T. Name another animal that has whiskers, like the lion.

S. The tiger.

T. Another, nearer home.

S. The cat.

T. Have you ever touched the cat's whiskers when she was dozing before the fire?

S. Yes; often.

T. And what did you notice?

S. It made her start.

T. What does that show?

S. That she feels keenly with her whiskers.

T. Can you give me one word for feeling keenly?

S. "Sensitive."

T. Well, then, here is one thing to remember: the cat's whiskers are very sensitive, and the lion's are the same. There

---

* From Socrates, a Greek philosopher, who made it his characteristic method of teaching. He died in 399 B.C.

are nerves of feeling at their roots which make him sensible of the very slightest touch; I therefore write on the board,—

> "The Lion's whiskers are sensitive."

Now, where are the lion's whiskers?
S. At each side of his mouth.
T. When a lion is walking on a plain, or through a wood, what part of him goes first?
S. His feet.
T. Think again.
SS. His head—His nose—His whiskers.
T. Right; his whiskers. And they not only go first, but they also—
S. Stretch out on both sides.
T. Right again. Now we have a second thing to write on the board,—

> "The Lion's whiskers are sensitive."
> "The Lion's whiskers go first."

Now, when you have to go across a dark room, or through a dark wood, what do you do?
S. We stretch out our hands.
T. Why?
S. To feel for things that may be in our way.
T. With what do you feel them?
S. With our fingers.
T. Why with your fingers?
S. Because they can go first.
T. Another reason.
S. Because they can feel keenly.
T. One word for that.
S. "Sensitive."
T. Where do the lion and the tiger go in the dark?
SS. Into the thick woods—Into the tangled jungle.

T. And have they fingers to stretch out?
S. No.
T. What have they instead?
S. Whiskers.
T. Now you know the use of whiskers to these animals?
S. To enable them to feel their way in the dark woods and jungle.

Probably the quicker witted scholars will have seen the teacher's drift long before the end has been reached; but they will not on that account follow the remaining steps of the process with the less interest. It should also be observed that the use of the questioning method is quite consistent with the preparation and use of Notes of Lessons. This is purely a question of method, which does not affect the arrangement or the selection of matter.

The young teacher should be warned to avoid "leading questions;" that is, questions which involve their own answers, and therefore require no thinking to answer them. Questions which may be answered categorically,—that is, with a simple "yes" or "no,"—ought also to be avoided. They do not throw any work upon the scholars, and they lead to guessing. Simultaneous answering is also objectionable. It causes confusion in the class, and it enables the ignorant to get credit for the knowledge of their neighbours.

Another kind of questioning, different from the above, and very useful in its place, is Examination questioning. Its object is not to convey instruction, but to test results. The time for it comes when the lesson, or the series of lessons, on a particular subject has been completed, and when the teacher wishes to ascertain how far his instructions have been mastered and remembered. Examination questions are generally more comprehensive than the questions used in teaching, and the answers to them are generally written down in the form of complete sentences or paragraphs.

EDUCATIONAL CATALOGUE.
1880.

The Royal School Series

SPECIMEN PAGES

OF

ROYAL INFANT SCHOOL SERIES.
ROYAL READERS. First, Second, and Third Series.
ROYAL HOME LESSON BOOKS.
ROYAL ARITHMETICS.
ROYAL GEOGRAPHIES.
WRITING EXERCISE BOOKS.
ROYAL HISTORIES.
&c. &c.

Thomas Nelson and Sons,
LONDON; EDINBURGH;
NEW YORK.

NEW INFANT SCHOOL SERIES. 1880.

NEW ROYAL PRIMER, Part II., containing Exercises on the Long Vowels, &c. Beautifully Illustrated. 32 pages. 1d. Cloth limp, 2d.

ship

sh	i	p
ch	i	p
wh	i	p

ship.　chip.　whip.

NEW INFANT SCHOOL SERIES. 1880.

NEW ROYAL PRIMER, Part II., containing Exercises on the Long Vowels, &c. Beautifully Illustrated. 32 pages. 1d. Cloth limp, 2d.

i · ip · ship.

1.
Ben will go in the ship.

2.
He cut a chip from a log.

3.
Tom has a top and a whip.

NEW INFANT SCHOOL SERIES. 1880.

"ROYAL" INFANT READER, containing general Exercises on the Vowel Sounds, with Reading Lessons in the form of simple stories and easy rhymes. Beautifully Illustrated. 64 pages. Cloth, 3d.

SAILING THE BOAT.

| boy | sea | mast | string |
| girl | boat | sail | bird |

1. Here are a boy and a girl wading in the sea.

2. The boy has his little boat with him. The boat has a mast and a sail.

NEW INFANT SCHOOL SERIES. 1880.

"ROYAL" INFANT READER, containing general Exercises on the Vowel Sounds, with Reading Lessons in the form of simple stories and easy rhymes. Beautifully Illustrated. 64 pages. Cloth, 3d.

3. He holds the boat with a string. The little girl says, "Blow, wind, blow; Make the ship go!"

4. The sea is very calm. Far off there is a sea-bird, high up in the air.

5. The little boy is called Fred. The little girl is his sister. Her name is Mary.

6. She has come to see Fred sail his boat. She likes to help him when she can.

7. Mary has always a smile on her face. At home she is called Little Sun-shine.

THE KETTLE AND ITS FRIENDS.

I AM a kettle. You have often seen me at work boiling water for your breakfast, dinner, or tea. Do you know what I am made of? I will tell you. I am made of iron; because iron will bear a great heat.

Here is my friend the coffee-pot. Do you know what he is made of? "No." Then I will tell you. My friend the coffee-pot is made of tin. He sometimes sits beside me on the hob. I often pour water into him hot enough to scald him, if he could only feel it.

Now you shall see a family of my friends. Without them I should not be so useful as I am.

FIRST SERIES.

ROYAL READER No. II. With Illustrations, Notes, Questions, Spelling Lessons, and Dictation Exercises, &c. 114 pages. 18mo, cloth. Price 7d.

THE TIGER.

THE TIGER.

Haunts, the places he frequents. | Prey, animals seized for food.
Hav´-oc, destruction; slaughter. | Vic´-tim, prey.

In India, there are vast tracts of waste land called *jungle*. The jungle is a part of the forest overgrown with tall thick grass and bushes. It is there chiefly that the tiger has his haunts.* There, by day as well as by night, he is on the watch for his prey.*

The skin of the tiger is covered all over with beautiful black stripes.

Though the tiger is very handsome with his beautiful striped skin, he is more fierce and cruel than any other creature that lives in the forest. People are even more afraid of him than they are of the lion. The lion is content with enough to satisfy his hunger, but the tiger is never satisfied. He tries to kill all he can, and dreadful is the havoc* he often makes.

FIRST SERIES.

ROYAL READER No. III. Illustrated. With Notes, Questions, Spelling Lessons, Dictation Exercises, and Useful Knowledge Lessons, &c. 192 pages. 18mo, cloth. Price 1s.

HOW A DOG GOT HIS DINNER.

HOW A DOG GOT HIS DINNER.

Cer′tain, fixed.
De-light′, joy; pleasure.
Guests, persons asked to the dinner.

Lib′er-al, free to give.
Re-ceived′, got.
Served, provided; treated.

IN a town in the south of France, twenty poor people were served* with dinner, at a certain* hour every day. A dog belonging to the place was always present at this meal, to watch for the scraps that were now and then thrown to him.

The guests,* however, were poor and hungry, and of course not very liberal.* So the poor dog hardly did more than smell the feast, of which he would have liked a share.

Now it happened that this dinner was served out to each one on his ringing a bell; but, as the person

FIRST SERIES.

ROYAL READER No. IV. Beautifully Illustrated. With Notes, Questions, Dictation Exercises, Composition Exercises, Word Lessons, and Outlines of British History. 288 pages. 18mo, cloth. Price 1s. 6d.

178   CROSSING THE ALPS.

cold. When half way up the mountains, a rumbling noise was heard among the cliffs. The guides looked at each other in alarm, for they knew well what it meant. It grew louder and louder. "An avalanche! an avalanche!" they shrieked; and the next moment a field of ice and snow came leaping down the mountains, striking the line of march and sweeping away thirty dragoons

FIRST SERIES.

ROYAL READER No. V. Beautifully Illustrated. With Notes, Questions, Dictation Exercises, Useful Knowledge Lessons, Choice Quotations, Biographies of Great Men, &c. 416 pages. 18mo, cloth. Price 2s.

188   THE SKATER AND THE WOLVES.

Every half minute a furious yelp from my fierce *attendants made me but too certain that they were in close pursuit. Nearer and nearer they came,—at last I heard their feet pattering on the ice—I even felt their very breath and heard their snuffing scent! Every nerve and muscle in my frame was stretched to the utmost tension.⁴

SKATER CHASED BY WOLVES.

The trees along the shore seemed to dance in an *uncertain light, and my brain turned with my own breathless speed; yet still my pursuers seemed to hiss forth their breath with a sound truly horrible, when an *involuntary motion on my part turned me out of my course. The wolves, close behind, unable to stop, and as unable to turn on the smooth ice, slipped and fell, still going on far ahead.

FIRST SERIES.

ROYAL READER No. VI. Illustrated. With Notes, Questions, Word Lessons, Dictation Exercises, Composition Exercises, Useful Knowledge Lessons, Biographical Appendix, Physical Geography, &c. 400 pages. 2s. 6d.

THE GREAT SIEGE OF GIBRALTAR. 15

a little before midnight, as did also D'Arçon, the French engineer, that on board of which he had embarked to witness the triumph of his ˙contrivances. Meanwhile, the most intense ˙anxiety as to the fate of Gibraltar prevailed in England. Admiral Howe had sailed from Portsmouth with a convoy containing fresh troops and provisions, and a fleet of thirty-four sail of the line. Relieved by the news of Elliot's ˙brilliant victory, which he received off the coast of Portugal, he steered direct for the Straits, and succeeded in bringing the whole of his transports to their ˙destination, even in presence of the enemy's fleets. Thus Gibraltar was saved, and the ˙continuance of the blockade till the peace (Jan. 20, 1783) was little more than a form.

accom´plish, perform´.
anni´hilated, destroyed´.
anxi´ety, solic´itude.
appli´ance, contriv´ance.
ar´maments, for´ces.
blockād´ed, invest´ed.
brill´iant, splen´did.
cannonade´, sustained´ fire.
cap´turing, seiz´ing.
com´petent, ad´equate.
contin´uance, prolonga´- tion.
contriv´ances, inven´tions.
convul´sively, spasmod´- ically.
deci´sive, fi´nal.

defi´ance, contempt´ for an enemy.
destina´tion, ha´ven.
destruc´tion, devasta´tion.
en´terprise, exploit´.
ex´ecuted, performed´.
for´midable, dān´gerous.
gigan´tic, stupen´dous.
im´minent, threat´ening.
import´ance, mo´ment.
inca´pable, una´ble.
inces´sant, cease´less.
inev´itable, unavoid´able.
inten´sified, made greater.
interrupt´, hin´der.
intrepid´ity, dâr´ing.

invin´cible, invul´nerable
ord´nance, can´non.
precip´itated, cast.
prod´igally, gen´erously.
recognized´, acknowl´edged.
reinforce´ments, fresh troops.
repulsed´, driven back.
requisi´tion, opera´tion.
resist´ance, defeat´.
slack´ened, declined´.
sor´tie, sally.
tremen´dous, overwhelm´- ing.
unprecedent´ed, unpar´al- leled.˙

[1] Gibral´tar.—Gibraltar is not so much a rocky fortress as a fortified mountain, with a town on one of its spurs. It occupies a remarkable tongue of land in the south of Spain, with which it is connected by a narrow neck of flat and neutral ground. The length of the peninsula from north to south is under three miles; its breadth nowhere exceeds three quarters of a mile. The north front of the rock rises perpendicularly from the neutral ground, and stretches across from sea to sea with the ex-

SECOND SERIES.

ROYAL READER No. I. With Illustrations, Spelling Lessons, &c. 96 pages. In leather-cloth. Price 4d.

70　　　　　　　MY NAME.

MY NAME.

1. A PIECE of the garden was marked off, and a border put round it, and George was told that it was to be his own little garden.

2. "But how will people know that it is mine?" he asked. "I cannot write my name on it."

3. "I can write your name on it," said his father; "and when we plant the seeds in the spring, I will do so."

4. Spring came, and his father got some seeds. Then he showed George how to make little beds, and how to sow the seeds in them.

5. When this had been done, George said, "But my name, father!—where is my name?"

SECOND SERIES.

R OYAL READER No. II. With Script Lessons, Dictation Exercises, &c. 168 pages. 18mo, cloth. Price 9d.

LIGHT-HOUSES.

LIGHT-HOUSES.

Gleamed, shone. | Piled, heaped up.
Hid-den, out of sight. | Warn, point out to.

1. THERE are rocks in the sea which are only a little way above water when the tide is low, and are quite covered when the tide is high.

2. Then ships are in great danger. In storms they are often dashed on these rocks, and broken in pieces, and the poor sailors are drowned.

3. The danger is greatest at night; for in the day-time the broken waves show where there are hidden* rocks. Light-houses are built on such rocks, to warn* sailors that danger is near.

4. "What is a light-house?" — A light-house is a house in the shape of a tall

90   SWALLOWS.

SWALLOWS.

1. THERE are some birds which do not live in England all the year round. When winter comes they fly away to warmer lands, and return again in spring. The swallow is one of these birds. It spends the winter in Africa, and does not come back to England until the month of March or April. It is a pleasant thing to see a flight of swallows at that

SECOND SERIES.

ROYAL READER No. IV. With Notes, Questions, Exercises, &c. 320 pages. 12mo, cloth. Price 1s. 9d.

SITTING AT MEAT IN THE EAST.   97

SITTING AT MEAT IN THE EAST.

1. 'ORIENTALS are far behind Western nations in almost every branch of 'domestic economy. The general custom even of the better classes at meals, is to bring a stool about fourteen inches high into the common sitting-room. On this stool is placed a tray of basket-work or of metal—generally copper—upon which the food is arranged.

2. Around this stool and tray the guests gather, sitting on the floor; or, in the case of rich families, 'reclining on soft, 'luxurious cushions, as shown in the picture. In Syria and Palestine the dishes are mostly stews of rice and beans, with soups or sauces held in deep dishes or bowls. Some use wooden or metal spoons for their stews and soups, but the most common mode is to double up bits of bread and dip them into the dish. This custom is frequently

SECOND SERIES.

ROYAL READER No. V. (For Standards V. and VI.)
12mo, cloth. 384 pages. Beautifully Illustrated. Price 2s.

100 ADRIFT ON AN ICE-FLOE.

from New London on the 3rd of July 1871. The progress made by the expedition was uneventful and unusually rapid. By the beginning of September they had reached lat. 82° 16'; and there they resolved to winter in a tolerably sheltered cove, about twelve miles long and nine miles wide, which Hall named "Thank God Harbour."

5. While preparations for "wintering" were being made, Captain Hall went on a sledge-journey On his return he fell suddenly ill. At first it was supposed to be only a temporary bilious attack, but on the following day the symptoms became alarming, and he was frequently

BURIAL OF CAPTAIN HALL.

delirious. His illness continued, and gradually assumed the appearance of paralysis, and early in the morning of the 8th of November the heroic explorer died.

6. Three days later, he was buried at noon by lantern-light, the coffin being hauled to the grave on a sledge, over

ROYAL HOME LESSON BOOKS for *First and Second Series* of Royal Readers. Nos. I. and II. 1d. each.—Nos. III. and IV. 2d. each.

ROYAL READER NO. III.—FIRST SERIES.

44.—THE DOG AT HIS MASTER'S GRAVE. [*Page 115.*]

1. low'-ly   tomb'-stone   start'-ed   skel'-e-ton   faint'-er
   mourn'-ful   gen'-tle   re-turn'-ing   chil'-dren   bro'-ken
   pit'-y-ing   pat'-ted   sum'-mer   win'-ter   strug'-gled
   of'-fer-ings fond'-ly   au'-tumn   an'-gry   mas'-ter
   bu'-ried   hâsten'-ing   de-cay'   moan'-ing   him-self'

2. SUMMARY.—A dog lay for months on his master's grave. When he heard the rustling of the grass, he started up, thinking it was the sound of his master's step. The children took him food, but they could not coax him to their homes. In winter he died.

3. An'-guish, very great grief. | Guard'-ed, kept watch over.
   Ca-ressed', made much of; fondled. | Heed'-ed, minded; noticed.
   Con-trolled', kept in check; ruled. | Mor'-tal, causing death; deadly.
   Fleet, flying very quickly. | Pleas'-ant-ly, in a kind way.
   Gaunt, wasted away; thin. | Quiv'-er-ing, shaking from strong feel-
   Grate'-ful, full of thanks. | ing; trembling.

4. *Write out twenty Nouns of the Masculine gender.*

45.—THE STONE THAT REBOUNDED. [*Page 116.*]

1. squal'-ling   fif'-ty   swal'-lows   trust'-ful-ly   peo'-ple
   prob'-a-bly   be-came'   măk'-ing   ut'-most   grand'-child
   pleas'-ant   coup'-le   win'-ter   sor'-ry   cru'-el-ty
   a-fraid'   Ham'-il-ton   re-turned'   mo'-ment   af-ter-wards
   un-der-stand' ev'-er-y-bod-y wel'-comed   noth'-ing   re-bound'-ed
   troub'-le   car'-ried   spok'-en   throw'-ing   deep'-ly

2. SUMMARY.—A boy thoughtlessly killed an aged couple's favourite bird with a stone. Her mate grieved very much for her, and the old people mourned for their bird. This made the boy so sorry, that he said the stone had rebounded and hit him.

3. Ac'-cu-rate, sure. | Pre-vent', stop; hinder.
   Con'-science, the power of know- | Reared, brought up.
   ing right and wrong. | Re-bound', spring back upon those
   In'-no-cent, harmless. {mind. | who threw it.
   Mem'-o-ry, the store-house of the | Re-joice', be very glad.
   Pois'-ing, balancing carefully. | Won't, will not.

4. *Learn the Time Table.*

THIRD SERIES.

ROYAL READER No. I. With Illustrations, Spelling Lessons, Script Lessons, &c. 96 pages, cloth. Price 6d.

THE CHILD AND THE SWALLOW.

THE CHILD AND THE SWALLOW.

1. One spring, two swallows built their nest just over the window of a room where a little boy named Arthur slept.

2. It was Arthur's great delight to watch the swallows flying about—out of the nest and in again, out and in, all day long.

3. No one touched the nest; and all the long summer the swallows made it their home.

4. At last the days began to grow shorter, the cold weather came, and the birds flew away to another land.

5. Arthur looked in vain for his little friends. His mother told him that they had gone to a warmer land far over the sea, but that they would come back when spring returned.

HORNS, TRUNK, AND TUSKS.

1. The cow has horns. Unlike the lion and the tiger, she has no claws with which to defend herself. Sometimes her horns are very long; but the cow is a gentle creature, and seldom attacks any one with them.

2. The horns of the cow are very useful. After death they are cut off. When soaked in boiling water they become soft. Then they may be moulded into any kind of shape.

HORNS.

3. Many common articles, such as buttons, combs, drinking-cups, and the handles of knives and forks, are made of horn.

4. The head of the elephant is unlike that of the cow, though both animals are grass-eaters. The elephant has a trunk, which takes the place of a nose, and also serves him as a hand. Here is a picture of an elephant's trunk.

TRUNK.

SHIPS.

8. The men who work a ship are called
_{8. The men hoo wurk a ship ar kawld}
sailors. When they wish to stop their vessel,
_{sail′-erz. Hwen thay wish to stop thair ves′-l,}
they throw out a
_{thay thrō out a}
large iron hook
_{lahrj ī-′ern hook}
called an anchor.
_{kawld an ang′-kor.}
Here is a picture
_{Heer iz a pik′-t'yūr}
of one.
_{ov wun.}

ANCHOR.

9. The anchor is fastened to one end of a
_{9. Thee ang′-kor iz fas′-nd to wun end ov a}
long rope or chain, the other end of which is
_{long rōp or chain, thee uth′-er end ov hwich iz}
fixed to the ship. When the anchor is caught
_{fikst to the ship. Hwen thee ang′-kor iz kawt}
in the ground, it keeps the ship from sailing
_{in the ground, it keeps the ship from sail′-ing}
away.
_{a-way′.}

10. A ship which is used in war is called a
_{10. A ship hwich iz yoozd in wawr iz kawld a}
man-of-war. It carries a number of large guns
_{man-ov-wawr′. It kar′-riz a num′-ber ov lahrj gunz}
or cannons, which are fired through holes in
_{or kan′-nunz, hwich ar fyrd throo hōlz in}
the sides of the vessel, called port-holes.
_{the sydz ov the ′ves-l, kawld pōrt′-hōlz.}

THIRD SERIES.

ROYAL READER No. II. *Pupil Teacher's Edition.* With the Correct Pronunciation of each Word interlined. Notes on Method, a Summary of the Chief Points in the Lesson, a Series of Questions, and a Note of Things to be Remembered in each Lesson. 8vo, cloth. Price 1s. 6d.

SHIPS. 75

sail′ing	steam′ers	pic′ture	cross′ing	cur′rants
car′ry	pad′dle	cov′ered	sug′ar	use′ful
car′ried	forced	paint′ed	cof′fee	an′chor
en′gines	pres′sure	con′stant-ly	rai′sins	caught

Chi′na, a country in Asia.
Greece, ⎫ countries in the south of Eu-
Spain, ⎬ rope where much fruit is
⎭ grown.
A-ra′bi-a, a country in Asia.

E′gypt, a country in Africa.
West In′dies, a group of islands off the coast of America.
Pas′sen-gers, persons who are travelling.

For Dictation, Composition, or Transcription.

SUMMARY.—Ships are built of wood or of iron. Some of them are moved along by means of the wind filling their sails, and others by means of steam-engines. The products of other lands are brought to us in ships. The men who work a ship are called sailors.

QUESTIONS.

1. What are ships made of?
2. Describe a sailing-ship.
3. Describe a steam-ship.
4. What are paddle-wheels?
5. How is a ship forced along by paddle-wheels?
6. For what are ships useful?
7. Mention some of the articles conveyed in ships.
8. How many passengers can be carried in the largest ships?
9. Describe a large ship, and mention some of the rooms in it.
10. Who are the sailors?
11. How do the sailors stop their ship?
12. What is an anchor?
13. What is a man-of-war?

THINGS TO BE REMEMBERED.

1. A sailing-ship is carried along by the wind, which fills its sails.
2. A steam-ship has engines which force it through the water.
3. A man-of-war is a ship which carries a number of soldiers, and is fitted up for use in times of war.

THE LAPLANDER. [Page 44.

METHOD.—Place the map of Europe before the class. Point out Lapland. Tell the children that the weather becomes colder and colder the further north you go. Describe the appearance of lands in the Arctic Circle. Refer to the long winters, and to the long period

WRITING EXERCISE BOOKS.

ARITHMETIC. SCHOOL SERIES. (*Graduated Course.*) Copy Book Size, Standards II., III., IV., V., VI. 2d. each. HOME SERIES. (*Test Questions.*) Pocket Size, II., III., IV., V., VI. 1d. each.

ARITHMETIC—STANDARD II.

(1.) *Multiply* **Twenty-six thousand three hundred and forty-eight** *by* **Five thousand and sixty.**

(2.) **James had three hundred nuts in his pocket; but there being a hole in it, he lost one hundred and eighteen nuts: how many had he left?**

(3.) *Multiply* **Three thousand five hundred and sixty** *by* itself.

(4.) *What is the difference between* **Six dozen dozen** *and* **Half a dozen dozen?**

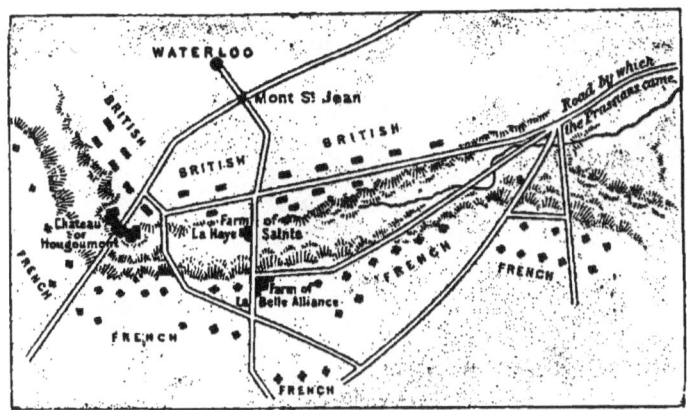

PLAN OF THE BATTLE-FIELD.

from the English guns. The French artillery replied; and then followed such a cannonade as had never been heard on battlefield before. The French battalions dashed on **Hougoumont**, which was held by the Guards. Round this chateau the battle raged furiously for hours. The French took the wood, broke the gate to pieces, but could not withstand the withering fire from the house, and the rain of shells from English howitzers.[1]

7. Marshal Ney led several columns against **La Haye Sainte**, and gained a temporary lodgment there, because the Germans had used all their ammunition; but their success came too late to be of any use. The circumstance which gave Waterloo a special character, was the trial of strength between the "rocky squares" of English infantry and the torrents of French horse. When the latter had almost spent their strength in frequent charges, nearly the whole of the English cavalry dashed at a sweeping gallop into the hollow, and literally rode over the lancers and cuirassiers, who had been vainly flinging themselves on the squares all day.

8. About four in the afternoon, the head of the **Prussian column** under Bulow began to emerge from the wood to the east. Menacing the right flank of the French position, they obliged Napoleon to risk his last desperate throw for the game,

---

[1] *Howitzers.*—Short, light cannon, capable of throwing heavy projectiles.

THE "ROYAL" CODE HISTORIES. — ENG-
LAND.—Part I. for Standard IV., price 3d.; Part II. for Standard V.,
price 6d.; Part III. for Standard VI., price 9d.

12   THE OLD ENGLISH KINGDOMS.   [449 A.D.

3. The Jutes[1] settled in Kent and on the Isle of Wight. The Saxons, from Holstein[2] and Friesland,[3] settled chiefly in the south. The Anglians, from Schleswig,[4] landed on the east coast and soon spread over the midland and northern districts, occupying most of the land. All these were kinsmen,—brothers, as it were, of the same family. They spoke the same tongue—English; they worshipped the same gods (chief of whom was Odin or Woden); and they were ruled by the same laws and customs. When they had made the land fairly their own, they called it after themselves, Englaland, England,—"the land of the English."

[1] *Jutes.*—By some the name *Jute* is held to be the same as *Geat;* that is, *Goth.* The name *Jutland* has no reference to land jutting. It means simply the land of the Jutes. *Wight* is probably the same word as *Geat* and *Jute.*

[2] *Holstein.*—A duchy of Germany (formerly of Denmark).

[3] *Friesland.*—In Holland; south and east of the Zuider Zee.

[4] *Schleswig.*—North of Holstein. Part of Schleswig is still called Anguln.

> GEOGRAPHY OF ENGLAND AND WALES.
> With Questions, Exercises, and 26 Maps. In paper cover, price 4d.; cloth, 6d.
> Also Geography of SCOTLAND, price 3d. The Geography of the COLONIES, price 4d.

COUNTIES AND CHIEF TOWNS.

COUNTIES AND CHIEF TOWNS.

The Towns are arranged from North to South. Names of Inland Towns are indented; the others are on the Coast. Asterisks indicate the County Towns.

NORTHERN DIVISION—ELEVEN COUNTIES.

On the Irish Sea .... Cumberland, Westmoreland, Lancashire, Cheshire.
In the Humber Basin.. York, Nottingham, Leicester, Stafford, Derby.
On the Tyne and Tees.. Northumberland and Durham.
Three Centres: NEWCASTLE, HULL, LIVERPOOL.

1.—NORTHUMBERLAND[1]—surface rugged; slopes from Cheviots and Pennine Chain to North Sea; coal and iron mines.

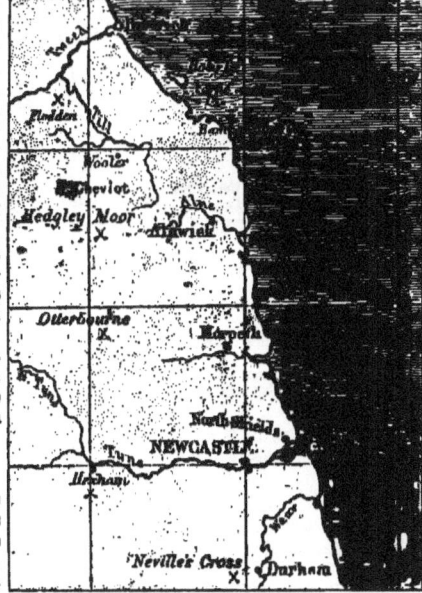

Berwick.
 Alnwick.
 Morpeth.
Newcastle.*
Nth. Shields.
Tynemouth.

Berwick-on-Tweed, the most northerly town in England, stands in a corner of Berwickshire called "The Liberties of Berwick." From 1551 till 1832 it was independent of both England and Scotland, but in 1832 it was included in Northumberland. At *Flodden Field*, on the Till, James IV. of Scotland was defeated and slain in 1513.
Alnwick (Alne); near it Malcolm Canmore was slain in 1093, and William the Lion was taken prisoner in 1174.
Morpeth, a market-town and railway junction.
 Newcastle, famous throughout the world for its coal. It is the centre of the largest coal-field in England, and is besides noted for the manufacture of machinery and glass. The town took its name from a "newcastle"

In this and the following maps, each complete square measures 20 miles each way.

built there by William the Conqueror. It has a wonderful high-level railway bridge, quarter of a mile long and 112 feet high; while 27 feet below the railway there is a carriage-road for ordinary traffic.
North Shields and *Tynemouth*, closely connected, have ship-building yards and coal exports. (Entire exports of coal from the Tyne, 5½ million tons a year.)

---

[1] *Northumberland*, the land north of the Humber. The old kingdom of *Northumbria* extended from the Humber to the Forth.

THE ENGLISH LANGUAGE: Its History and Structure. 12mo, cloth limp. Price 7d.

Designed to meet the requirements of the Education Codes in regard to the History and Structure of the English Language, to Paraphrasing, and to Composition of Sentences.

CHART OF THE ENGLISH LANGUAGE AND ENGLISH LITERATURE.

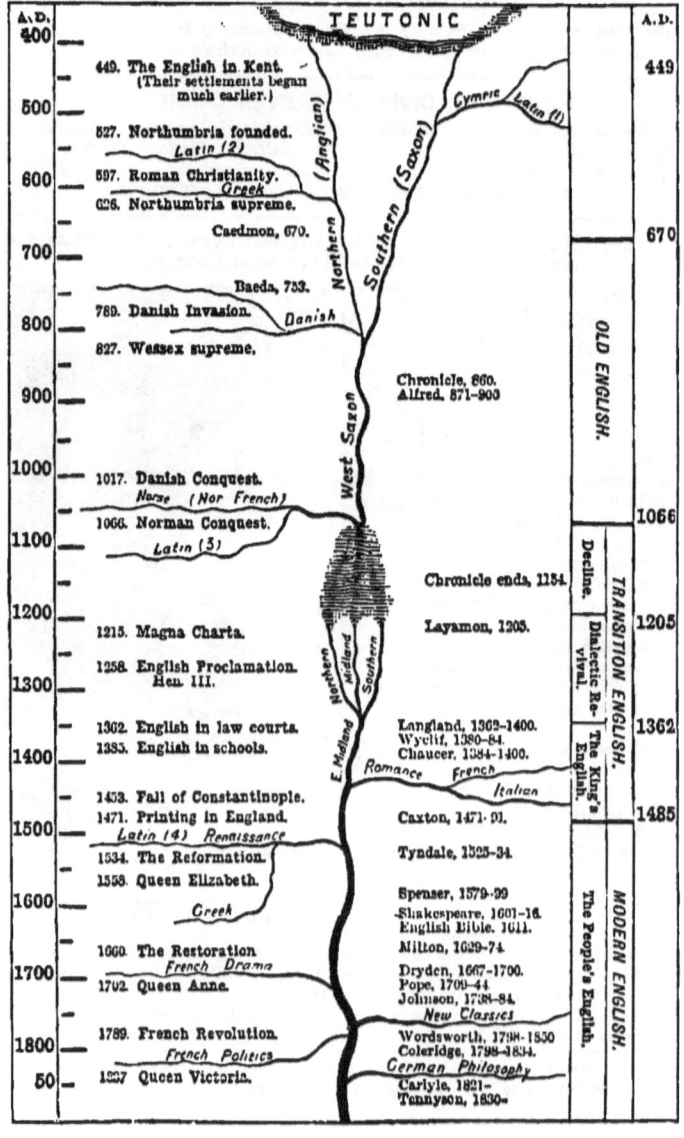

> THE ENGLISH LANGUAGE: Its History and Structure. 12mo, cloth limp. Price 7d.
> Designed to meet the requirements of the Education Codes in regard to the History and Structure of the English Language, to Paraphrasing, and to Composition of Sentences.

XIII.—THE TRANSITION TIME.
DECLINE AND REVIVAL.
1066-1362 A.D.

OUTLINE.—1. For more than a century after the Conquest, English was in a state of decline (1066-1205).——2. This was followed by a time of dialectic revival (1205-1362).——3. The chief writers of that time were Layamon (1205) and Ormin (1215).——4. During that time the Norman-French were absorbed in the English people.——5. The characteristics of Transition English are the simplification of grammar, and the addition of few Norman-French words.

1. For more than a century after the Conquest, English was in a state of **decline**; that is to say, as has already been shown, it ceased to be a book speech, and became a spoken or "illiterate" tongue. In this state it continued till about the year 1205. The changes which it underwent during that time were not so much due to the direct influence of Norman-French, as to English having been driven into obscurity and deprived of literary practice and a literary standard.

2. When English **reappeared** as a book speech, its form was greatly changed; rather, it appeared in several forms, differing materially from one another. This was the natural consequence of the want of a literary standard. In different parts of the country change had taken different directions, and had resulted in **different forms.**

In the thirteenth and fourteenth centuries there were three distinct dialects in which books were written,—the **Northern**, the **Midland**, and the **Southern.** These dialects are most readily distinguished by the plural ending of the present tense, which was in the Northern -es, in the Midland -en, and in the Southern -eth. The Northern dialect was spoken in the Lowlands of Scotland as well as in the north of England, and passed into modern Lowland Scotch. The Southern dialect was a continuation of the classical tongue of Wessex; but it gradually died out. The Midland dialect was a revival or a development of the English of the Peterborough Chronicle (1154), and afterwards passed into standard English.

MODEL NOTES OF LESSONS. For Class Teaching.
A Manual of Method, and a Collection of Models on the Subjects commonly taught in Elementary Schools. For the Use of Pupil Teachers and of Students in Training Colleges. Post 8vo, cloth. 128 pages. Price 2s.

NOTES OF LESSONS ON ANIMALS.

MODEL LESSON: THE LION.

Articles required.—*Pictures of Cat and Lion—Map of World.*
INTRODUCTION.—Show pictures of Cat and Lion, and ask questions to bring out their likeness.

HEADS.	MATTER.	METHOD.
CLASSIFICATION.	Division.—Back-boned.	Contrast with worm, snail, and star-fish.
	Class.—Mammals.	Explain literal meaning: "suckling its young." Contrast with birds and fishes.
	Order.—Flesh-eaters	Contrast with cow and horse.
	Family.—Cat tribe	Give examples: cat, tiger; and ask for others.
STRUCTURE.	Body.—Long—strong, compact bones—powerful muscles—tawny skin	Point to each part of animal when describing it. Get description from the class.
	Size.—Height, about 4 feet—length, about 7 feet	Show lengths on schoolroom wall.
	Head.—Round	Compare with cat.
	Eyes.—Large, round—able to see in dark	Show use, in seeking prey by night. (See HABITS.)
	Teeth.—Sharp-pointed	Show use, in tearing flesh. (See FOOD.)
	Tongue.—Rough	Show use, in scraping flesh off bones. (See FOOD.)
	Neck.—Very strong	Illustrate by story of a lion carrying off an ox.
	Mane.—Long—on male only	Compare with horse's mane.
	Whiskers.—Extend sideways from mouth	Show use, in enabling it to feel its way through the jungle.
	Feet.—Padded under each toe	Show use, when approaching its prey.
	Claws.—Sharp—sheathed in pad	Compare with sword and its sheath.
	Tail.—Long, tufted	Compare with tassel.
HABITS and QUALITIES.	Sleeps during day—lies in wait near water at night, and springs on animals as they drink—fierce—cunning—fond of young.	Compare with cat watching for mice, and its mode of catching them.
FOOD.	Beast of prey—deer, sheep, oxen, sometimes men.	Refer to STRUCTURE and HABITS.
LOCALITY.	Africa, India, Persia. Asiatic lion smaller than the African.	Show countries on map.
USES.	Skins used for rugs.	Tell a lion-story: hunted with elephants, &c.

> MODEL NOTES OF LESSONS. For Class Teaching.
> A Manual of Method, and a Collection of Models on the Subjects commonly taught in Elementary Schools. For the Use of Pupil Teachers and of Students in Training Colleges. Post 8vo, cloth. 128 pages. Price 2s.

NOTES OF LESSONS ON ANIMALS.

COMPARISON OF ANIMALS.

THIS table contains Outline Lessons on a Quadruped, a Bird, and a Fish, arranged on the same plan, in order to show that the model may be adapted to any animal. The student should be asked to construct a similar skeleton of lessons on other animals, say the Elephant, the Shark and the Spider. By this means he will become thoroughly acquainted with the structure of the lesson.

Arrangement of Lesson.	HORSE.	OSTRICH.	COD.
INTRODUCTION	Refer to daily use.	Refer to Peacock.	Ask for names of well-known fishes.
CLASSIFICATION.	Division.... Back-boned. Class...... Mammals. Order...... Thick-skinned.	Division.... Back-boned. Class...... Birds. Order...... Runners.	Division.... Back-boned. Class...... Fishes. Order...... Bone-skeleton.
STRUCTURE.	Size—colour—form of body— kinds.	Size—colour—form of body— wings—feathers—legs—feet.	Size—colour—form of body— jaws—teeth—fins.
HABITS and QUALITIES.	In a wild state lives in herds— fleet-footed—very timid.	Lives in flocks—quick of hearing —acute smell—fleet-footed.	Haunts shallow water—spawns in cold seas.
FOOD.	Vegetable: grass—hay—corn— beans.	Vegetable: shrubs—young plants —seeds—almost any kind.	Small 'fish—worms—crabs and other small shell-fish.
LOCALITY.	In nearly all parts of the world— found wild in South America, in Tartary, and in Africa.	In deserts of Africa.	Chiefly in seas of temperate regions. Very abundant off Newfoundland and Nova Scotia.
USES.	As a domestic animal, is sagacious, obedient, and faithful— skin is used for leather—hoofs for glue—hair for cushions.	Valuable feathers—flesh eaten— eggs used.	Food — very prolific — 15,000 British seamen employed in the cod-fishery.

www.ingramcontent.com/pod-product-compliance
Lightning Source LLC
Chambersburg PA
CBHW022123160426
43197CB00009B/1130